Help, I Can't Stop Laughing!

a nonstop collection of life's funniest stories

Books by Ann Spangler

Don't Stop Laughing Now! compiled by Ann Spangler
and Shari MacDonald
Fathers of the Bible, Ann Spangler with Robert Wolgemuth
Look Who's Laughing! compiled by Ann Spangler
and Shari MacDonald
Men of the Bible, coauthored with Robert Wolgemuth
Mothers of the Bible, Ann Spangler with Jean Syswerda
Praying the Names of God
She Who Laughs, Lasts! compiled by Ann Spangler
Women of the Bible, coauthored with Jean Syswerda
Women of the Bible: 52 Stories for Prayer and Reflection

Help, I Can't Stop Laughing!

a nonstop collection of life's funniest stories

selected by
Ann Spangler
with Shari MacDonald

ZONDERVAN™

GRAND RAPIDS, MICHIGAN 49530 USA

ZONDERVAN.COM/
AUTHOR**TRACKER**

ZONDERVAN™

Help, I Can't Stop Laughing!
Copyright © 2006 by Ann Spangler

Requests for information should be addressed to:
Zondervan, *Grand Rapids, Michigan 49530*

Library of Congress Cataloging-in-Publication Data

Help, I can't stop laughing! / selected by Ann Spangler and Shari MacDonald.
   p. cm.
   ISBN-13: 978-0-310-25954-1
   ISBN-10: 0-310-25954-1
   1. Religion—Humor. 2. Conduct of life—Humor. I. Spangler, Ann. II.
MacDonald, Shari.
PN6231.R4H45 2005
817'.6080382—dc22   2005022237

Interior design by Michelle Espinoza

Printed in the United States of America

---

06 07 08 09 10 11 • 18 17 16 15 14 13 12 11 10 9 8 7 6 5 4 3 2 1

Contents

Chapter Six: It's All in How You Look at It (and Laugh at It)

Chapter Seven: Kid Stuff

Chapter Eight: Dad's a Hoot!

Chapter Sixteen: Can't Stop Laughing

Chapter Seventeen: Laughing All the Way

Preface

James Langston Hughes, a noted African American poet, once commented: "Like a welcome summer rain, humor may suddenly cleanse and cool the earth, the air, and you." Of course he is describing the kind of humor that is neither mean-spirited nor cynical, the kind Shari and I have done our best to include between the covers of this book. By sharing some of our favorite stories, one-liners, and jokes, we hope to offer you a source of continual refreshment in the midst of life's struggles and stresses. Like the person who wisely advised that "Every survival kit should include a sense of humor," Shari and I hope you will consider *Help, I Can't Stop Laughing!* an essential tool in your own survival kit.

Some of the funniest stories we have come across are the true-life tales people tell on themselves — life's most embarrassing moments that provoke laughter for years to come. We hope that as you read these, you will give in to the temptation to laugh at yourself from time to time and that you will become comfortable regaling friends and family members with your own set of life's "most embarrassing moments."

While we were working on the book, I confess to having my fill of embarrassing moments. Of these, one in particular stands out. It happened one day when I decided to ease my stress level by indulging in a massage. After sixty minutes of being kneaded, pummeled, and stroked, I felt a tremendous sense of relief and peace. All was well with my world — at least for the next couple of hours. To top it off I felt a surge of confidence when my therapist, at the end of the massage, inquired whether I might be a swimmer. Concluding that she must have deduced this information from working on my well-toned muscles, I proudly responded, that, yes, I kept fit by swimming two or three times a week. "I knew it!" came her triumphant reply. "I can always tell the swimmers because their skin smells like chlorine!"

Humor is a powerful weapon against our vainglory. It is also a tonic for our souls. So whether or not life seems funny or sad or somewhere in between, Shari and I hope that you will make humor a steady part of your life by reading and sharing the stories in this book. If you like them, you might be interested to know that this is the fourth in a series of similar books, all of which are designed to keep you laughing through life's ups and downs: *She Who Laughs, Lasts! Don't Stop Laughing Now*, and *Look Who's Laughing.*

As with our previous books, we want to express our gratitude to the authors whose work this book includes. Without them there would be no peals of laughter, no chuckles too great to suppress. Their stories encourage all of us to keep laughing even and especially when life gets tough. Thanks too to the many publishers who have given permission to use material in this book.

Special thanks go to our editor, Sandy VanderZicht, a woman who laughs easily and contagiously, and to Lucinda Poel for so carefully and patiently making corrections to the manuscript. Thanks to Sue Brower and Sherry Guzy and their fellow marketers at Zondervan, who have done so much to spread the laughter by supporting this and previous books in the series.

To you the reader — we wish you many happy moments, whether you are lying in bed, sitting in your favorite easy chair, or stretched out on a towel at the beach. We hope you will read the stories, share them with friends, and then make laughter a part of your lifestyle, always on the lookout for reasons to laugh, taking as your motto this epitaph from an unknown source: "Love is my sword, goodness my armor, and humor my shield."

1

If Image Were Everything, We'd Be in Big Trouble

Honest criticism is hard to take, particularly from a relative,
a friend, an acquaintance, or a stranger.

— Franklin P. Jones

I refuse to think of them as chin hairs.
I think of them as stray eyebrows.

— Janette Barber

Clothes make the man. Naked people have little
or no influence on society.

— Mark Twain

Wild Mama
Rachael Phillips

Sleeping in — an unknown luxury, a fairy-tale fantasy that inevitably dissolved in a shower of Cheerios and the wiggles and jiggles and messy, precious kisses of my preschoolers. Sleeping in existed in a different solar system — or perhaps in a different galaxy far, far away.

But those thoughts evaporated as I lay in a bed I wouldn't have to make, savoring the ecstasy of a quiet — yes, quiet — sixteenth-story hotel room. My husband had already left for his conference, and I indulged in forbidden pleasures: a cup of real coffee (double cream) in bed, steaming hot from the first mellow sip to the very last; a television program in which most people already knew how to count to ten; and a long, sinful bath filled to the top, with no Mr. Bubble or rubber duckies in sight.

After bathing, I ignored my ratty plaid bathrobe hanging on the hook. I didn't decide what to wear. Instead, I wandered around the room, carefree and content as Eve in the Garden of Eden, unhampered by diaper bags, car seats, nap times, or must-have blankies. I pondered how I would spend an entire day without children or Happy Meals. Intoxicated with my liberty, I forgot my mother's advice to always close the drapes and faced the room-sized picture windows. The panoramic view of city streets and smaller buildings far below dazzled my eyes, my soul. Embracing the endless azure sky, I sang, "I'm free! Free!"

"Chuk-chuk-chuk-chuk-*chuk*!" A dragonfly the size of a sixties Cadillac suddenly hovered by the window. I hit the floor as if attacked by enemy fire, yanking the bedspread (too late!) across my naked, prostrate form. The traffic helicopter pilot waved. Then he and his mighty machine swept off to corners of the universe where other derelict mothers in need of reform might lurk.

I pulled the blanket over my head and groaned. Mortification stuffed my throat like a giant spoonful of crunchy peanut butter. I felt a hot strawberry flush from my toes to my eyebrows. Not counting God, only my husband and my doctor had seen me in the buff; now a nameless helicopter pilot in Cleveland shared that … er … privilege.

Him and who else? I grabbed my heart and my ratty plaid bathrobe and edged toward the window. Praise be. No Blue Angel precision jet formations screaming into view, scouting for the Miss Thunder Thighs competition. I closed the drapes, then donned a pair of khakis and my highest-necked sweater. I started my makeup routine. No blush needed today!

I didn't dare turn the radio on as usual. Couldn't bear to think of that friendly pilot's nine o'clock traffic report. "*Great* view over the city," he'd say. "Why, I can see clear to next Tuesday. No accidents downtown, but hey, cover up — er, buckle up! — for safety, and slow down for those curves!"

Or maybe he'd give a few cute weather tips: "Sunny, but chilly. Dress in layers. At least *one*."

Maybe They're Just Young at Heart
David L. Reese

During our annual Hymn Fest Sunday, we normally pit the women against the men or one section of voices against another. But this year we pitted those who are fifty-four and younger against those who are fifty-five and older.

We all sang the first two verses of music quite well. However, on verse three, when it was time for the fifty-five and older group to sing, you could hear only the male voices. The men were amazed at how many of our senior women suddenly became "fifty-four and younger."

The Truth Hurts
Various Authors

I met my six-year-old son at the bus one day after I'd gotten a new haircut. Although it felt great, my new look had the effect of making my already substantial nose seem even more prominent. The next morning I awoke to Julian softly running his fingers across my face, clearly deep in thought. "Mom," he asked seriously, "did you tell a lie?"

— Sally R.

And keep a sense of humor. It doesn't mean you have to tell jokes. If you can't think of anything else when you're my age, take off your clothes and walk in front of a mirror. I guarantee you'll get a laugh.

— Art Linkletter

Imagination was given to man to compensate him for what he is not; a sense of humor to console him for what he is.

— Francis Bacon

Adorable, Schmorable!
Julie Ann Barnhill

I was standing in line at the bank one summer morning with about twelve other customers and my eighteen-month-old daughter. The lobby was bustling with customers, all waiting for overstressed tellers who would have preferred to be out sunbathing rather than giving change to yet one more customer.

The banking center had an open design that made all the personal bankers privy to the comings and goings of staff and customers. In addition, the bank managers had their offices along the perimeter of the building, each enclosed with glass walls that afforded every titled employee a front-row seat to any banking spectacles, such as the one I was about to present. I was third in line, and little Kristen was standing directly behind me. She sported a cute summer outfit with a large red strawberry motif on the shirt and tiny baby strawberries on the matching shorts. Her silky dark brown hair fell just to her shoulders and drew up into bouncy tendrils that framed her chocolate brown eyes. Her smooth olive complexion and mischievous expression caused more than one fellow spectator to exclaim, "How adorable!"

I had delivered my second child, Ricky Neal, about three weeks before, and I was sporting the appropriate clothing for one who had, until recently, been very pregnant. My oversized T-shirt, knotted loosely at my hips, strategically camouflaged the results of having carried a nine-pound, eight-ounce bundle of joy. The black, stretchy Capri leggings, accented at the calves with a wide band of lace, did their best not to give away evidence of the Oreo cookie raids preceding his birth.

While Kristen and I waited in line, she entertained the captive audience with such feats as spinning around until she was dizzy, scrunching her nose and lips to make an obnoxious breathing sound through her nostrils, and making faces at the people behind us. I, of course, felt delighted to have such a cute and precocious child.

I had moved up to second in line when Kristen started to turn her attention toward me.

Her mother. The woman who had agonized fourteen hours, surviving on ice chips alone, to bring her into this world.

She began to focus her attention — all eighteen months' worth — on me. The woman who thought the sun rose and set on her, this precious child.

"Next," said the teller.

I stepped to the window and plopped the proceeds of a weekend garage sale on the marble countertop. The proceeds consisted of $717.83 — mostly in quarters, nickels, and three pennies.

I glanced back to check on Kristen and then rested my elbows on the countertop, leaning forward and relaxing, just taking it easy and thinking how I was going to spend all that money.

This is the point where Kristen directed her attention fully to me.

I felt a small, tentative poke on my, er, backside.

I ignored it.

Bad decision.

Then another small — but decidedly stronger than the first — poke against my backside, accompanied by a singsong voice proclaiming, "Big bottom, Mom! Big bottom!"

Poke, poke. Prod, prod.

I whipped around and saw my three-foot munchkin grinning from ear to ear. Bolstered by the smiles and chuckles from those in her immediate vicinity, she kept poking and declaring. I lowered my head, unknotted my shirt, and whispered delicately, "Kristen, stop poking Mommy — and quit saying 'big bottom.'"

She appeared to understand what I was saying, so I continued, "It isn't nice to talk about Mommy's bottom. Now don't say 'bottom' again."

I turned back to Teller Girl, who was trying to quell a smirk, with dismal results.

Not a peep was heard from behind me.

Good.

Uh, scratch that. The silence following my little chat with Kristen was not good. She had used those brief moments for thinking, and now the small poke flourished into an all-out punch. With her tiny yet accurate pointer finger aiming for the rear, Kristen proclaimed for everyone, teller and glass-ensconced manager alike, to hear: "Big butt, Mommy, big butt!"

Is it any wonder I have issues?

Oh, Baby!
Rachael Phillips

ut I think you're beautiful."
I stared at my husband with incredulous pity. What insanity
had blinded his usual astute vision? Seven months pregnant with
our first child, I felt like a walking ottoman. Even my earlobes felt
puffy and heavy, like overripe fruit clinging to a tree. My stomach
was the size of a state fair blue ribbon watermelon, so monumental
and taut I feared it would crack if it grew any bigger.

"Turn around." Steve gave me a gentle push. "Look in the mirror. See? From the rear, you can't even tell you're pregnant."

"So if I just walk backwards, nobody will know?" I had spent
the last hour soaking in a warm, luxuriant pool of self-pity, and I
rather liked it.

He chuckled. "It means you'll lose the weight fast after the
baby's born." A resident physician in a family practice program at
the local hospital, Steve knew how to handle cranky women in their
last trimester.

I kissed him good-bye. My part-time shift at a small Christian
college started in a couple of hours. Would I splurge and take the
bus, or ride my bike through our quiet neighborhood, as I had continued to do throughout my pregnancy? I grinned. Each time I
tootled up on my secondhand three-speed, Mr. Plunkett, an older
man in the office where I worked, threw his window open in horror.
"Mrs. Phillips!" he shouted. "What are you *doing*? Come inside this
instant and put your feet up!" He always brought me a glass of cold
water and flapped over me like an indignant pelican. Where was my
mother? Did my husband *really* find this acceptable?

I had a great job.

But the graying skies made the prospect of a bike ride a little
riskier than usual. Mr. P. might have a coronary if I rode up amidst
thunder and lightning. I decided to take the bus. I finished the laundry

and put on my pink maternity outfit (I owned two, and I'd worn the other one with the blue stripes the day before). I slipped into the comfortable new sandals I'd bought when I could no longer see my feet or tie shoelaces. Toting a big umbrella, I arrived at the bus stop a couple of blocks away. I checked my watch. Five minutes. I drifted into a reverie of nursery rhymes and rock-a-by songs.

"Hey, Pink Pants!" masculine voices called over my shoulder. A long whistle echoed through the air, then another. "Hey, baby! Oh, BABY!"

I stared at my stomach, confused. Sure, I was going to have a baby, but ...? I cast a cautious glance behind me. Two linemen, perched like vultures on the top of a telephone pole, hooted at me. And yes, unless I had lost my feminine instincts along with my waistline, ear-to-ear lecherous smiles gleamed on their faces, simmered in their eyes.

Blank disbelief washed over me — then a joyous rush of wickedness that almost compensated for feeling fat. But Niceness pointed a finger at me, and I wavered. Should I? Or shouldn't I?

I turned around, pursed my lips in a Valley Girl smile, and waved sweetly at my admirers, who nearly fell to the ground. Then I waddled up the steps onto the bus. As it rolled away, I watched them hugging the pole, trying in vain to hide scarlet guilty faces.

"Whoa, baby," I whispered to my stomach. "You're already knocking 'em off their feet."

"Pledging" Her Love
Michele Howe

Ⓢ

Before leaving for a dinner engagement, sixty-year-old Donnie Meyers decided her husband Phil's hair needed fixing. Grudgingly, he allowed her to recomb it and apply some hair spray.

Driving to their destination, the two noticed a peculiar smell in the car, which lingered the entire evening.

Arriving home, Donnie checked the expiration date of the hair spray. When she found the can, the mystery was solved — she had mistakenly sprayed furniture polish on Phil's hair. She went to another room and enjoyed a private laugh, knowing that some things are better left unsaid.

The Spitting Preacher
Mark Lowry

Y ears ago, on a hot Sunday morning in a little country church, I performed a twenty-minute concert before the pastor got up to speak. I took a seat on the front row, where I normally sit when I am a special guest in a church. The front row is a great place to observe body language, facial expressions, and hair transplants. I noticed, however, that everybody else was sitting in the back, but it was a Baptist church, so I didn't think much about it. In this little church, the front row was just a few feet away from the pulpit. From where I was sitting, I could count the lines in the pastor's forehead.

It wasn't bad when he started, and I was really enjoying his sermon. He could really preach, but I didn't hear him finish because he did something that distracted me.

The pastor was preaching on *Yeshua Hamashiach* (Hebrew for "Jesus, the Messiah"), but he had a little trouble saying it. I think he had hyperactive spit glands, because the more excited he became, the harder they worked.

In the middle of his sermon, he raised his Bible in the air, slammed his fist down on the pulpit, and sprayed, "*Yeshua Hamashiach* is the Lord!"

It looked as if Niagara Falls had broken loose.

I couldn't believe what I was seeing. The man was spitting all over the place. I felt like I was riding a pew through a car wash. It's a wonder he didn't electrocute himself with that much water hitting the microphone. Every time he opened his mouth, he showered another section of the congregation. He was an equal-opportunity spitter, and the louder he preached, the thicker the mist.

I wanted to look away. His cascading saliva was making me feel nauseous. But I couldn't. I knew if he should happen to look at me and see me looking as if I wasn't paying attention, he might not give me a good love offering, and then I wouldn't be able to eat and buy gas so I could get to the next town and sing for another spitting preacher.

So I continued to look at him.

He was drooling like a rabid dog. Frothing at the mouth like that demon-possessed man Jesus healed in the graveyard.

The room started spinning, and I realized that I had to get out of there. But he'd only said "in closing" twice, so I knew we had twenty more minutes. I started repeating over and over to myself, *Stare at his forehead! Don't look at his mouth! Stare at his forehead! Don't look at his mouth!*

But you know me, I never listen. My eyes were drawn to the saliva puddling around his tongue, splashing over his bottom lip. Every time his lips separated, little strings as thin as fishing line would stretch, snap, and land somewhere on the pulpit.

On some syllables he actually blew bubbles. Why did I forget my umbrella again?

At this point, I'd forgotten what he was preaching about. But he hadn't. Through the flying confetti, I could see his hands flailing and hear his voice rising. The sermon had gone on so long I wondered if he'd ever run out of spit. How much of that stuff can a body produce in an hour? I tried to get my mind off the falling saliva and onto what he was saying, but then I noticed a change. The air seemed to be clearing. The floating particles were landing and fortunately none on me. His hyperactive spit glands had finally been depleted ... and all was well. Except now his tongue was dry and he was having trouble pronouncing his *S*s. By the time he said, "Shall we stand and sing a song of salvation, saints?" I could barely understand him.

At the end of the service, the pastor took me to lunch. He handed me a check and asked me what I thought of his sermon — and if I had any advice for him.

I said, "I only have one word of advice, and I don't know if you'll get it."

"Try me," he said.

I said, "Okay. Here's my advice: Swallow."

People in Glass Houses ...
Connie Pettersen

I cringed when my elderly mother removed her coat in the church entryway prior to a formal family wedding. To my dismay, her outfit rivaled my daughters' attempts at dressing themselves when they were four. Mom's casual polyester cream and lavender checked slacks clashed with a white and purple print blouse.

I rolled my eyes at my sister-in-law, Jane, who also noticed the unusual combinations, then leaned over and whispered, "'When I am old, I shall wear purple.'" Jane grinned and nodded in agreement.

The wedding was about to start, so we took our places in church. It wasn't until I put my purse under the pew that I saw how unqualified I was to give fashion advice.

I had on two mismatched brown shoes.

2

Church Chuckles

*There are four classes of church members: the tired,
the retired, the tiresome, and the tireless.*

— Anonymous

A church is a place where you encounter nodding acquaintances.

— Anonymous

Quit griping about your church; if it were perfect you couldn't belong.

— Msgr. Joseph P. Dooley

I Just Dropped Back In to Mention One Last Thing
Brandon Moody

In the Easter cantata at the church my uncle pastors, the climactic scene was the ascension. In this sequence, the actor playing Christ was to be slowly hoisted out of view through an opening in the ceiling.

"Lo, I am with you always," he said, signaling for the "ascension" to begin. "Even unto the end of the world."

The flight upward was progressing smoothly, until the stage crew briefly lost grip of the rope and the actor nearly dropped back to the stage. With enviable stage presence, he remained in character as his feet dangled inches from the floor and his bewildered disciples looked on in horror.

"Oh, and one more thing," he said calmly. "Love one another."

Immediately, the rope yanked him up into the ceiling and out of sight.

Bulletin Bloopers
Anonymous

- Jean will be leading a weight-management series Wednesday nights. She's used the program herself and has been growing like crazy!

- This afternoon there will be a meeting in the South and North ends of the church. Children will be baptized at both ends.

- Tuesday at 4:00 p.m. there will be an ice cream social. All ladies giving milk will please come early.

- Wednesday the ladies liturgy will meet. Mrs. Johnson will sing "Put Me in My Little Bed" accompanied by the pastor.

- The service will close with "Little Drops of Water." One of the ladies will start quietly and the rest of the congregation will join in.

- The ladies of the church have cast off clothing of every kind. They can be seen in the church basement Saturday.

- The Lutheran men's group will meet at 6:00 p.m. Steak, mashed potatoes, green beans, bread, and dessert will be served for a nominal feel.

- Eight new choir robes are currently needed, due to the addition of several new members and to the deterioration of some older ones.

- The senior choir invites any member of the congregation who enjoys sinning to join the choir.

- At the evening service tonight, the sermon topic will be "What Is Hell?" Come early and listen to our choir practice.

- Today ... Christian Youth Fellowship Sexuality Course, 8:00 p.m. Please park in the rear parking lot for this activity.

- The eighth graders will be presenting Shakespeare's *Hamlet* in the church basement on Friday at 7:00 p.m. The congregation is invited to attend this tragedy.

- The associate minister unveiled the church's new giving campaign slogan last Sunday: "I Upped My Pledge — Up Yours."

- A new loudspeaker system has been installed in the church. It was given by one of our members in honor of his wife.

Fuel for Faith
Dan Clark

Two nuns were driving down a country road when they ran out of gas. They walked to a farmhouse and a farmer gave them some gasoline, but the only container he had was an old bedpan. The nuns were happy to take whatever they were offered and returned to their car.

As they were pouring the gasoline from the bedpan into the tank of their car, a Protestant minister drove by. He stopped, rolled down his window, and said, "Excuse me, sisters. I'm not of your religion, but I couldn't help admiring your faith!"

To Tell the Truth
Gracie Malone

As the story goes, an old farmer went to the city one weekend and attended the big-city church. When he came home his wife asked him how it was.

"It was good," said the farmer, "but they did something different. They sang praise choruses instead of hymns."

"Praise choruses?" asked his wife. "What are those?"

"They're sort of like hymns," the farmer said, "but they're different in some ways."

"Well," his wife persisted, "what is the difference?"

"The best way I can explain it is like this," the farmer said. "If I were to say to you, 'Martha, the cows are in the corn,' well, that would be a hymn. If, on the other hand, I said to you, 'Martha, Martha, Martha, oh, Martha, Martha, Martha! The cows, the big cows, the brown cows, the black cows, the white cows, the black and white cows, the cows, cows, cows, are in the corn, are in the corn, are in the corn,' well, that would be a praise chorus."

Distracted
Mark Buchanan

Iassume that you're like me: I can get itchy-skinned and scratchy-throated after an hour or so of church. I can get distracted and cranky when it goes too long. My feet ache, my backside numbs, my eyes glaze, my mind fogs, my belly growls. I find myself fighting back yawns, and then not fighting them back, letting them gape and roar, a signal to my oppressors: *Let my people go*.

And I'm the pastor.

What Do They Say When They're Playing "House"?
Kathleen Eakin

Our three small children announced one evening that they were going to "play church." We were pleased and proud at the same time.

We ate humble pie, though, when we spied them running around in a panic, pretending to get dressed, and yelling, "Hurry up!" "It's time for church!" "We have five minutes!" "We'll be late!"

We're More Divided Than We Thought

Anonymous

A woman went to the post office to buy stamps for her Christmas cards. "What denomination?" asked the clerk. "Oh, good heavens! Have we come to this?" said the woman. "Well, give me fifty Catholic and fifty Baptist ones."

Church Feuds
Anonymous

Church feuds are not uncommon, especially among cliques in the congregation. But when the pastor and choir director get into it, stand aside.

One week, our preacher preached on commitment and how we should dedicate ourselves to service. The director then led the choir in singing "I Shall Not Be Moved."

The next Sunday, the preacher preached on giving and how we should gladly give to the work of the Lord. The choir director led the song "Jesus Paid It All."

The next Sunday, the preacher preached on gossiping and how we should watch our tongues. The hymn was "I Love to Tell the Story."

The preacher became disgusted over the situation, and the next Sunday he told the congregation he was considering resigning. The choir then sang "Oh, Why Not Tonight?"

When the preacher resigned the next week, he told the church that Jesus had led him there and Jesus was taking him away. The choir then sang "What a Friend We Have in Jesus."

Laughter Isn't the Only Thing That's Contagious
Clara Null

When I lived in a small town in Mississippi, I heard that the local Baptist minister got a phone call from a teenager whose mother was very ill.

"Brother John," he said, "Mother wants you to come pray with her."

The Baptist minister was flattered since he knew the family attended the Church of Christ. But he had to ask, "Is Brother Syms [the Church of Christ minister] out of town?"

"No, sir," the boy said. "We don't want Brother Syms exposed to what Mother has."

We Thought It Was the Holy Spirit
Harry Grob

ⓔ

Our minister usually delivered his sermons without too much dramatic flair. But one Sunday as he was speaking, he suddenly exclaimed, "My goodness!" hopped from one side of the pulpit to the other, then pounded the top of the pulpit twice with his Bible.

Stunned at first, the congregation quickly responded with plenty of amens, vigorous nods, and applause.

After composing himself, our pastor finished the sermon and came down to greet church members. When my turn came, I complimented him for his lively sermon. He whispered back, "You'd have jumped around too if that black widow spider had come after you!"

"Dear Lord ..."
Anonymous

❧

A visiting minister offered the opening prayer: "Dear Lord," he began with arms extended and a rapturous look on his upturned face, "without you we are but dust ..."

He would have continued, but at that silent, awkward moment when he paused for a breath, one very obedient young girl (who was listening carefully) leaned over to her mother and asked quite audibly in her shrill little voice:

"Mommy, *what* is butt dust?"

Church was pretty much over at that point ...

Fun with Furry and Feathered (Even Scaly and Creepy) Friends

A man who carries a cat by the tail learns something he can learn in no other way.

— Mark Twain

Sign in pet store: "Buy One Dog, Get One Flea."

— Anonymous

A real Christian is the one who can give his pet parrot to the town gossip.

— Billy Graham

Kitty Flight
Anonymous

We like the inspirational version of this popular story.
A pastor had a kitten that climbed up a tree in his backyard but then was afraid to come down. The pastor coaxed, offered warm milk, and so on. The kitty would not come down. The tree was not sturdy enough to climb, so the pastor decided that if he tied a rope to his car and drove away so that the tree bent down, he could then reach up and get the kitten. He did all this, checking his progress in the car frequently, then figured if he went just a little bit farther, the tree would be bent sufficiently for him to reach the kitten. But as he moved a little farther forward, the rope broke. The tree went *boing,* and the kitten instantly sailed through the air — out of sight.

The pastor felt terrible. He walked all over the neighborhood asking people if they'd seen a little kitten. No. Nobody had seen a stray kitten. So he prayed, "Lord, I just commit this kitten to your keeping," and went on about his business.

A few days later he was at the grocery store and met one of his church members. He happened to look into her shopping cart and was amazed to see cat food. Now this woman was a cat hater and everyone knew it, so he asked her, "Why are you buying cat food when you hate cats so much?"

She replied, "You won't believe this," and told him how her little girl had been begging her for a cat, but she kept refusing. Then a few days before, the child had begged again, so the exasperated mom finally told her little girl, "Well, if God gives you a cat, I'll let you keep it."

She told the pastor, "I watched my child go out in the yard, get on her knees, and ask God for a cat. And really, Pastor, you won't believe this, but I saw it with my own eyes. A kitten suddenly came flying out of the blue sky, with its paws spread out, and landed right in front of her!"

Where Did Mama Go?
Karen Scalf Linamen

Harald called me yesterday with a story that will send any arachnophobics among my readership into therapy.

Harald is my brother-in-law. He and my sister Renee live in Oak Harbor, Washington, with their three boys, six goldfish, and a tarantula.

The tarantula is a new addition. One week ago, their family roster did not include a spider the size of carry-on luggage.

It all started when my sister Renee decided to go away for the weekend for a women's retreat. As she was heading out the door, her husband announced that he would be taking the boys to the pet store because seven-year-old Hunter wanted to buy a pet. Harald added, "He wants a tarantula."

"Absolutely no tarantulas," Renee said. "If a spider like that ever got loose in the house, I'd have to move into a hotel. No Best Western, either. I'm talking Hilton."

The next day Harald and the boys were driving in the van, Hunter cradling a glass terrarium on his lap, when Harald said, "Oh, yeah. Don't let it get loose in the house or Mom'll have to move to a motel or something."

They arrived home and carried their furry friend into the house. Less than an hour later, one of the boys was holding the terrarium when it fell to the floor and broke into tiny pieces. Harald spied the eight-legged wonder sitting dazed among the glass. He rushed to pick it up. The spider promptly bit Harald's finger. Harald flung the spider to the ground, where it scurried under a kitchen cabinet.

Harald looked at the clock.

Renee was due home in two hours.

Armed with a flashlight and broomstick, Harald probed the small hole into which the black spider had fled. No luck.

Returning from the garage, Harald plugged in a 6.5 horsepower Shop Vac capable of suctioning the dimples off Joe Namath. But it couldn't dislodge an arachnid from a cabinet.

Undaunted, Harald headed back to the garage. When he returned a few minutes later, he was brandishing an electric saw.

By now several neighborhood husbands had learned of the crisis and gathered round to offer hearty masculine support as, piece by piece, Harald began sawing apart his cabinets. The cabinet floor beneath the sink went first. Then various kick plates. Then bottoms of drawers.

They finally found the tarantula in the last possible section of cabinet.

The furry interloper was safely imprisoned in a borrowed terrarium when Renee walked in the front door.

She immediately said, "What happened here?"

Harald said, "Why do you ask?"

"There's a seventy-five-pound Shop Vac sitting on the white carpet in the middle of the living room, that's why. What's going on?"

The men in my sister's life — all four of them, from the midlifer down to the preschooler — looked her in the eye and said, "Nothing. Nothing happened. Everything's fine."

Around the corner in the kitchen, the cabinets lay in pieces, and sawdust was still settling around the flashlights, saws, and Shop Vac attachments.

I imagine Renee was about to figure it out on her own. She didn't have to. Hunter confessed. Then, to make up for all the commotion his pet had caused, he decided to do something extra special for his mom.

He named the spider in her honor. He named it "Mama."

We can learn a lot from this story. We can learn to avoid women's retreats, staying home instead to protect our homestead from well-meaning husbands and venomous spiders larger than most of our body parts.

Renee says that, besides the women's retreat thing, the experience is also teaching her to face her fears. She says, "I don't want to steal Hunter's joy over this pet. So I'm working on putting aside my fears. I make a conscious effort to go look at the tarantula at least once an hour, sometimes twice, just to desensitize myself. Not to mention to make sure he's still in his cage."

Sort of like living with Hannibal Lecter.

I wish you and I could be protected from everything that goes bump in the night. Instead, we have a God who says, "Yes, they'll go bump, but let me hold the flashlight, and we'll face it together."

And who knows? When it's all said and done, maybe we'll come out ahead, in possession of things we couldn't have gotten any other way, things like mettle and strength and spirit. Not to mention an eight-inch-long spider named "Mama."

Dogs and Cats
Anonymous

Ꙩ

Adam and Eve said, "Lord, when we were in the garden, you walked with us every day. Now we do not see you anymore. We are lonesome here, and it is difficult for us to remember how much you love us."

And God said, "No problem! I will create a companion for you who will be with you forever and who will be a reflection of my love for you, so that you will love me even when you cannot see me. Regardless of how selfish or childish or unlovable you may be, this new companion will accept you as you are and will love you as I do, in spite of yourselves."

And God created a new animal to be a companion for Adam and Eve.

And it was a good animal.

And God was pleased.

And the new animal was pleased to be with Adam and Eve, and he wagged his tail.

And Adam said, "Lord, I have already named all the animals in the kingdom, and I cannot think of a name for this new animal."

And God said, "No problem. Because I have created this new animal to be a reflection of my love for you, his name will be a reflection of my own name, and you will call him *Dog*."

And Dog lived with Adam and Eve and was a companion to them and loved them.

And they were comforted.

And God was pleased.

And Dog was content and wagged his tail.

After a while, it came to pass that an angel came to the Lord and said, "Lord, Adam and Eve have become filled with pride. They strut and preen like peacocks, and they believe they are worthy of adoration. Dog has indeed taught them that they are loved, but perhaps too well."

And God said, "No problem! I will create for them a companion who will be with them forever and who will see them as they are. The companion will remind them of their limitations, so they will know that they are not always worthy of adoration."

And God created *Cat* to be a companion to Adam and Eve.

And Cat would not obey them.

And when Adam and Eve gazed into Cat's eyes, they were reminded that they were not the supreme beings.

And Adam and Eve learned humility.

And they were greatly improved.

And God was pleased.

And Dog was happy.

And Cat didn't give a fig one way or the other.

The Well
Anonymous

Two good ole boys were out walking. They passed through a meadow where the grass was about knee-high. It became apparent that the meadow was an old junkyard. There were old engines, rusted fenders, and used appliances lying about.

Suddenly, they came across a large hole. It looked very deep.

"How deep do you think it is?" said the first.

"I don't know," said the second.

"Let's push this old transmission into the hole and see how far she drops," said the first.

With much effort, the two good ole boys finally pushed and shoved the junky transmission to the edge of the hole and over the edge. After quite some time they heard a faint *splash*.

"Man, that is some deep hole," one of them said.

As soon as he said this, a billy goat came running out of the nearby woods just as fast as he could go, ran right past the good ole boys, and dived straight into the hole.

Flabbergasted, the two good ole boys stood there looking at each other, speechless.

A farmer appeared from the woods and asked them, "Have you seen my billy goat? He was somewhere around here, but it looks like he's run off. He couldn't have gotten far. I had him tied to an old transmission."

Rules for Cats
Anonymous

ⓔ

BATHROOMS: Always accompany guests to the bathroom. It is not necessary to do anything. Just sit and stare.

DOORS: Do not allow any closed doors in any room. To get door open, stand on hind legs and hammer with forepaws. Once door is opened, it is not necessary to use it. After you have ordered an "outside" door opened, stand halfway in and out and think about several things. This is particularly important during very cold weather, rain, snow, or mosquito season.

CHAIRS AND RUGS: If you have to throw up, get to a chair quickly. If you cannot manage in time, get to an Oriental rug. If there is no Oriental rug, shag is good. When throwing up on the carpet, make sure you back up so it is as long as a human's bare foot.

HAMPERING: If one of your humans is engaged in some activity and the other is idle, stay with the busy one. This is called "helping," otherwise known as "hampering." Following are the rules for "hampering":

1. When supervising cooking, sit just behind the left heel of the cook. You cannot be seen and thereby stand a better chance of being stepped on and then picked up and comforted.
2. For book readers, get in close under the chin, between eyes and book, unless you can lie across the book itself.
3. For paperwork, lie on the work in the most appropriate manner so as to obscure as much of the work as possible or at least the most important part. Pretend to doze, but every so often reach out and slap the pencil or pen.
4. For people paying bills or working on income taxes or Christmas cards, keep in mind the aim: to hamper! First, sit on the paper being worked on. When dislodged, watch sadly from the side of the table. When activity proceeds nicely, roll

around on the papers, scattering them to the best of your ability. After being removed for the second time, push pens, pencils, and erasers off the table, one at a time.

5. When a human is holding the newspaper in front of him/her, be sure to jump on the back of the paper. Humans love to jump.

6. When human is working at computer, jump up on desk, walk across keyboard, bat at mouse pointer on screen, and then lie in human's lap across arms, hampering typing in progress.

WALKING: As often as possible, dart quickly and as close as possible in front of the human, especially on stairs, when they have something in their arms, in the dark, and when they first get up in the morning. This will help their coordination skills.

BEDTIME: Always sleep on the human at night so he/she cannot move around.

LITTER BOX: When using the litter box, be sure to kick as much litter out of the box as possible. Humans love the feel of kitty litter between their toes.

HIDING: Every now and then, hide in a place where the humans cannot find you. Do not come out for three to four hours under any circumstances. This will cause the humans to panic (which they love), thinking that you have run away or are lost. Once you do come out, the humans will cover you with love and kisses, and you will probably get a treat.

ONE LAST THOUGHT: Whenever possible, get close to a human, especially their face, turn around, and present your butt to them. Humans love this, so do it often. And don't forget guests.

Unwelcome Guests
Mark Buchanan

The summer I wrote this, we discovered a nest of snakes living in our house. It was a hot spell, and often we retreated to the basement to escape the worst of it.

We weren't the only ones, it turned out.

A mother snake, at some point, had found her way into our house (we left most of our doors open that summer to create airflow). She had slithered into the back corner of the coolest, most interior room, and there hatched a brood of baby snakes: tiny black serpents, with slender, tapered bodies and teardrop-shaped heads and little red flickering tongues.

I hate snakes. I once heard about a man who, digging in his garden, hacked his shin apart with his spade when a garter snake slithered up his pant leg. I understood this: the panic, the wildness, the madness, the willingness to maim yourself to protect yourself. If it had been me and not Adam and Eve in Eden, we wouldn't be in the trouble we're in, but not because I have greater virtue; simply because it was a *serpent* who seduced them. I'd have killed it first.

One evening I came home from a deacon's meeting (was this itself a sign?) and Cheryl, wide-eyed and pale, met me at the door. "We have snakes," she said, hissing and writhing, snakelike herself. She and my son had already managed to jar two of the babies. It was my job, I was told, to track down the mother. I began with stiff caution, jabbing sticks under furniture, then leaping back, expecting Medusa's head to come shaking out at me. Everything I rousted out — a wisp of dust, a stray hairpin, a snip of thread — startled me. Every sensation of something touching me — the edge of a quilt brushing my shin, the corner of a desk biting my hip, a strand of cobweb trailing across my neck, the frays of cut cloth tickling my arm — sent me into a spasm of thrashing. After a while, I got bolder, more determined, especially since I had looked everywhere and found nothing.

"She's gone," I said. "Must have got out somehow. She's a bad mother. Abandoned the little ones to their fate. Imagine that."

Cheryl wasn't buying it. "Check again," she said. "Take a better look under the hide-a-bed. Mark, I spend hours in this room every week. My parents are coming on Monday to sleep in this room. I won't rest until I know it's safe."

So I pulled the mattress off the hide-a-bed and poked my head under the frame.

Bingo.

There she was, curled up on the back ledge of the bed frame. She was only about fourteen inches long and no thicker than my baby finger. But in my phobic, manic alertness, she may as well have been a Burmese python, smugly swallowing the dog, just getting started.

What followed was ten minutes of slapstick comedy — a burlesque of blundering, scrambling antics, a wild pantomime of overreaction. I chased that snake around, trying to pinch its thin, wriggling body between two blunt-end four-foot sticks and drop it into a small-mouthed jar. It kept getting free, to the accompaniment of our shrieks and hollers, and would scoot off to another corner and pile its body into dense coils. After several tries, it was glaringly obvious this approach was futile. I asked my son to fetch my garden gloves. I would have to pick it up.

I did it. There was no heroism or elegance in it. I held the snake away from me like I might a dead fish that had been left out in the sun. But I did it.

Over the next few days, as we found more snakes, we discovered that our nine-year-old daughter Sarah was fearless with them. She would simply pick up each snake with her bare hands, hold it near her face, scold it as though it were a naughty dog who had chewed up the hose, then set it loose in the garden, telling it to go find its mother.

Here's the thing. Ever since, it's been hard for me to rest in that room. Walking into it, I slow, halt, turn, look now this way, now that. I even look up, as though I'm dealing with a fat, hungry tree snake, its body languidly draped along the curtain rod, its head undulating downward. Every nerve in me is heightened, every muscle taut and trembling, and the little hairs on my arms stand up.

I may never sleep in that bed again. After we found the snakes, we had a string of stifling hot nights — nights like huge furnaces, roaring and devouring, the surface of things glazed with heat. Nights that skewered and roasted you like a pig on a spit, turning slowly, dripping, shriveling. On nights like those, we used to escape to the coolness of the basement to sleep.

But no more.

Instead, we now suffer upstairs, suffer all night long. There we lie, listless and restless, prickly and sweaty, longing for relief. On the worst of these nights I almost give in, slip downstairs, open the hide-a-bed, and crawl in. But I know it's no good. Every time I shut my eyes, I would see them, thousands of them, every length and thickness of them, twining, coiling, darting, hissing, squirming. I know that if I ever got to sleep's threshold, to that blissful, hypnotic place where your body hovers over oblivion and starts to ease down, something would graze the nape of my neck or tickle the hollow in my collarbone, and I would leap up, wild with panic, punching the air and slapping myself.

I don't trust that bed.

As fate would have it, I (Ann) was a guest of the Buchanans' a couple of months after the incident described above. Not having read Mark's story yet, I had no idea that my host had consigned his honorable guest to — you guessed it — the infamous hide-a-bed!

The Difference between Dogs and Cats
John Ortberg

According to received wisdom, there is a difference between dogs and cats. A dog says, "You love me, feed me, shelter me, care for me — *you* must be God." A cat says, "You love me, feed me, shelter me, care for me — *I* must be God."

Dead Duck
John William Smith

M y son Lincoln and I were heading home after a very successful fishing trip. It was cold and dark. We were speeding
along a narrow, twisting country road when suddenly my head-
lights revealed a white piscovey duck in the middle of the road. I
couldn't imagine what it was doing in the road at that time of night.
I thought ducks were like chickens and went to sleep as soon as it
got dark — and this one should have. I was going much too fast to
swerve, and there was no time to stop. I heard the sickening *whack*
and *crunch* of the duck hitting the underside of the car repeatedly.

It isn't easy to explain my next action — in fact, it's a little
embarrassing — but I have to try, or I can't tell the rest of the story.
You need to know me personally, and you need to understand the
way I was brought up. In my family nothing was ever wasted. It was
a sin to waste.

I turned around and went back to pick up the duck so we could
take it home and eat it. It was lying in a heap, sprawled out in obvious death in the middle of ten thousand feathers. I pulled up along-
side, reached out my door, picked up the duck, laid it on the floor
behind my seat, and headed home once again. I was driving a compact car. It was an Opel with bucket seats.

My son was very quiet as we drove, but completely alert. Normally, he would have been sound asleep after such a day, but the incident with the duck had totally captured his imagination. I noticed
that he kept looking behind my seat. A few minutes later, he said,
"Dad, do ducks have souls?"

"No, Son, ducks don't have souls."

"What happens to a duck when it dies?"

"We eat it."

"I mean, where does it go?"

"It doesn't go anywhere. It just *isn't* anymore."

"Oh." He thought for a few minutes, and then he said, "Dad, is it okay to pray for a duck?"

"I guess so, but why would you want to?"

"I feel sorry for it."

He lapsed into a thoughtful silence, and I assumed that he was praying. He kept his eyes on the duck, and a few minutes later he spoke again.

"Dad?"

"What, Son?"

"God just answered my prayer; that duck's alive."

"God doesn't do things like that anymore. The duck is dead."

A few minutes passed.

"Dad? Why doesn't God do things like that anymore?"

"Because the age of miracles has ceased."

"Dad, are you sure of that? The duck is alive. I just saw it move."

"No, Son, the duck may have moved from the motion of the car, but that duck is not alive. I know you feel sorry for the duck, and I do too, and I know you prayed for the duck, but we have to learn to accept bad things in life. *The duck is dead.* You heard it hit the car, didn't you?"

"Yes, but, Dad, the duck just moved again, and it's not the motion of the car. *It's looking right at me.*"

"Son, this has gone far enough. You mustn't allow your imagination to run away with you. I've told you that the duck is dead. *It is dead!* No amount of wishful thinking can bring it back. Trust me. I'm your father, and when *I* tell you that the duck is *dead*, you can believe me. *The — duck — is — dead!* Now, I don't want to hear any more about that duck; do you understand?"

"Yes, sir."

Quack.

"What was that noise?"

"I think it was the dead duck, Dad."

I turned around, and sure enough, there was the duck, standing up and looking rather puzzled by its new surroundings.

"Son," I said, "the age of miracles just started again, because that duck was dead!"

We took it home, fed it, found a marvelous place for it to stay — in our swimming pool, which was closed for the winter anyway — and we named her (I guess it was a her) Gertrude.

I learned a lesson from Gertrude the duck that day. I learned that I'm not always right. I learned that older isn't always wiser; I learned that sometimes we allow our presuppositions to override obvious facts; and I learned that if I insist on being right and won't even *listen* to another point of view, I might be forced to acknowledge my fallibility by a loud "Quack" of reality.

The next time you feel compelled to stand your ground no matter the facts, just remember Gertrude the duck and relax a little. Learn the grace of laughing at yourself.

It really isn't so bad to admit that you're wrong once in a while.

4

Just for Kicks and Giggles

Laughter is the sun that drives winter from the human face.

— Victor Hugo

Funny Bumper Stickers
Anonymous

- It IS as bad as you think, and they ARE out to get you.
- I love cats ... they taste just like chicken.
- Out of my mind. Back in five minutes.
- I get enough exercise just pushing my luck.
- Montana — at least our cows are sane!
- I didn't fight my way to the top of the food chain to be a vegetarian.
- Where there's a will, I want to be in it.
- I don't suffer from insanity, I enjoy every minute of it.
- IRS: We've got what it takes to take what you've got.
- Time is the best teacher; unfortunately it kills all its students.
- Give me ambiguity or give me something else.
- Make it idiot-proof and someone will make a better idiot.
- Always remember you're unique, just like everyone else.
- Consciousness: that annoying time between naps.
- There are three kinds of people: those who can count and those who can't.
- Ever stop to think and forget to start again?

Speeding
Anonymous

◉

A police officer pulls a guy over for speeding and has the following exchange:

Officer: "May I see your driver's license?"

Driver: "I don't have one. I had it suspended when I got my fifth DUI."

Officer: "May I see the owner's card for this vehicle?"

Driver: "It's not my car. I stole it."

Officer: "The car is stolen?"

Driver: "That's right. But come to think of it, I think I saw the owner's card in the glove box when I was putting my gun in."

Officer: "There's a gun in the glove box?"

Driver: "Yes, sir. That's where I put it after I shot and killed the woman who owns this car and stuffed her in the trunk."

Officer: "There's a BODY in the TRUNK?!?!?"

Driver: "Yes, sir."

Hearing this, the officer immediately called his captain. The car was quickly surrounded by police, and the captain approached the driver to handle the tense situation:

Captain: "Sir, may I see your license?"

Driver: "Sure. Here it is." It was valid.

Captain: "Whose car is this?"

Driver: "It's mine, Officer. Here's the owner's card." The driver owned the car.

Captain: "Could you slowly open your glove box so I can see if there's a gun in it?"

Driver: "Yes, sir, but there's no gun in it." Sure enough, there was nothing in the glove box.

Captain: "Would you mind opening your trunk? I was told you said there's a body in it."

Driver: "No problem." Trunk is opened: no body.

Captain: "I don't understand it. The officer who stopped you said you told him you didn't have a license, stole the car, had a gun in the glove box, and that there was a dead body in the trunk."

Driver: "Really? Ain't that something? And I'll bet that liar told you I was speeding too."

How to Get Time Off from Work
Anonymous

Two factory workers were talking. "I know how to get some time off from work," said the man. "How do you think you will do that?" said the woman. He proceeded to show her ... by climbing up to the rafters and hanging upside down.

The boss walked in, saw the worker hanging from the ceiling, and asked him what on earth he was doing. "I'm a lightbulb," answered the guy.

"I think you need some time off," said the boss. So the man jumped down and walked out of the factory. The second worker began walking out too. The boss asked her where did she think she was going.

"Home. I can't work in the dark."

Insurance Claims — Short Responses
Anonymous

- Coming home, I drove into the wrong house and collided with a tree I don't have.

- I collided with a stationary car going the other way.

- A pedestrian hit me and went under my car.

- I had been shopping for plants all day and was on my way home. As I reached an intersection, a hedge sprang up, obscuring my vision, and I did not see the other car.

- To avoid hitting the bumper of the car in front, I struck the pedestrian.

- My car was legally parked as it backed into the other vehicle.

- An invisible car came out of nowhere, struck my car, and vanished.

- I was sure the old fellow would never make it to the other side of the curb when I struck him.

- I was thrown from the car as it left the road. I was later found in the ditch by some stray cows.

- The telephone pole was approaching. I was attempting to swerve out of its way when it struck the front end.

Kids and Science
Anonymous
©

- When they broke open molecules, they found they were stuffed with atoms. But when they broke open atoms, they found them stuffed with explosions.

- When people run around and around in circles, we say they are crazy. When planets do it, we say they are orbiting.

- Most books now say our sun is a star. But it still knows how to change back into a sun in the daytime.

- A vibration is a motion that cannot make up its mind which way it wants to go.

- Many dead animals of the past changed to fossils; others preferred to be oil.

- Some people can tell what time it is by looking at the sun. But I have never been able to make out the numbers.

- We say the cause of perfume disappearing is evaporation. Evaporation gets blamed for a lot of things people forget to put the top on.

- I am not sure how clouds get formed. But the clouds know how to do it, and that is the important thing.

- In making rain water, it takes everything from H to O.

- Rain is saved up in cloud banks.

- Thunder is a rich source of loudness.

- Isotherms and isobars are even more important than their names sound.

- It is so hot in some parts of the world that the people there have to live other places.

Things You'd Rather Not Hear During Surgery

Anonymous

(ᴄ)

- Better save that. We'll need it for the autopsy.

- Someone call the janitor — we're going to need a mop.

- Wait a minute. If this is his spleen, then what's that?

- That's cool! Now, can you make his leg twitch?

- Well, folks, this will be an experiment for all of us.

- Sterile, schmerile. The floor's clean, right?

- And now we remove the subject's brain and place it in the body of the ape.

True Comments from Actual Employee Performance Reviews
Anonymous

- Since my last report, he has reached rock bottom and has started to dig.

- His men would follow him anywhere but only out of morbid curiosity.

- I would not allow this employee to breed.

- This employee is really not so much of a has-been but more of a definitely won't-be.

- Works well when under constant supervision and cornered like a rat in a trap.

- When she opens her mouth, it seems that this is only to change whichever foot was previously in there.

- He would be out of his depth in a parking lot puddle.

- This young lady has delusions of adequacy.

- She sets low personal standards and then consistently fails to achieve them.

- This employee should go far — and the sooner he starts, the better.

- This employee is depriving a village somewhere of an idiot.

- A gross ignoramus — 144 times worse than an ordinary ignoramus.

- When his IQ reaches fifty, he should sell.

- Donated her brain to science before she was done using it.

- If you give him a penny for his thoughts, you'd get change.

5

The Mind Is a Terrible
Thing to Waste

My mind not only wanders, sometimes it leaves completely.

— Barbara Johnson

The word genius *isn't applicable in football. A genius is
a guy like Norman Einstein.*

— former MVP quarterback Joe Theismann

"Mentalpause"
Mary Pierce

I called American Express last week to fix an error on our bill. The customer service rep put me on hold while she made the correction. When she came back on the line, she said, "Thank you for waiting. This is what I did ..." She paused for several long moments and then said, "Now what was it I did?" She laughed. I laughed.

"I understand," I said. "It's been such a long time since you did it."

She laughed again. "Yes, I'm having a senior moment ..."

Just the other day, I started to tell my twenty-something daughter a story and she stopped me midsentence. "You already told me that story. Yesterday," she said. I was mortified. This was something *old* people did!

"It's okay, Mom," she said. "I understand. It's mentalpause."

Senior moments. Mentalpause. Old-timer's disease. I'm sick of hearing about those things. And I'm tired of all those Internet lists: "Fifty Ways to Know You're Over Fifty" and the "How You Know You're Old" jokes. "My back goes out more often than I do." "I get winded playing video games." I'm sick of it all!

We're all getting older. Do we need to keep reminding each other? Oh, sure, it's all funny, in a "misery loves company" sort of way. But enough is enough!

Maybe it's all just payback. I used to laugh at my mother for absentmindedly putting the milk in the cupboard and the saltshaker in the refrigerator. Now I do the same things. Last week I misplaced the dog. She ran into the garage as I was unloading groceries. I locked her out there. Four hours later, Terry asked where she was. I looked at him blankly, thinking, *Do we have a dog?*

"Dog?" I said. "I don't know. She was here a minute ago, wasn't she?" I was sure I'd just seen her trot through the kitchen.

The other day I searched for my half-slip, digging through dresser drawers, rummaging through the hamper. It was nowhere to be found. I was wearing a heavy skirt, so I decided I'd just go without the slip. Before leaving the house, I stopped in the bathroom. As I was readjusting myself, I found the slip. Right there under my skirt. I'd been wearing it all along. Sad thing is, I'd already looked there once.

One morning last week, I chased our car down the driveway in my robe and slippers, waving and hollering at my departing husband. When I caught up to the car, he stopped and lowered the car window. I panted, "You'd better not leave without kissing me good-bye!"

"I'd be glad to kiss you again, but I just did. By the microwave. Five minutes ago."

This has nothing to do with his kissing. This has everything to do with my mind.

What is happening to my mind? My life has become a journalism exercise — answering the five *W*s and the *H*. *What was I just saying? Where did I leave the dog? When did we get a dog? Why did I come into this room? Why did I get down on my knees — to pray or to clean the dust from under the bed? Who is this woman in the mirror? When did she lose her grip? How did I get to this sorry state?*

"With age comes wisdom." That's a lie, at least in my case. The longer I live, the less I know, due to a combination of factors. One is "brain fog." Facts that once were clear and prominent are now hidden under a blanket of fog that's settled in the valleys between the ridges of my cerebral cortex. It's like any other fog bank: you know the ground is still there, but darned if you can see it anymore.

Then there's the harsh reality that I've murdered gazillions of brain cells watching reruns on Nick at Nite. (June Cleaver still wears her pearls with every single outfit, just in case you're curious and don't have cable.) Another gazillion brain cells have voluntarily leapt out my ears in a desperate effort to save themselves from having to think my increasingly stupid thoughts. *Should I switch to Country Blossom air freshener or stick with Tahitian Spice? Should I wear the plaid top with the green skirt, or the red top with the blue skirt? Where is my half-slip?* These are the deep things I ponder. I hear my brain cells muttering as they pack their bags, "You'd think just ONCE she'd contemplate world peace or quantum physics, but noooo ..."

So age has not brought wisdom. Between the brain cells jumping ship and the fog over the rest of the harbor, navigating the waters of life gets tougher by the day. The longer I live, the less I know. (Did I tell you that already? Or can't you remember either?) But the good news is I'm less aware that I don't know it. (If that made sense to you, you are obviously younger than I am.)

I missed a meeting a few weeks back. A meeting I had called. A meeting other women had to arrange child care to attend. A meeting I was supposed to be leading. I sat in my office that morning, thinking how nice it was to have some free time. I glanced at the clock. *9:30? Oh, NO! I was supposed to be at that meeting at 8:00!*

I know what you're thinking. I should have reminded myself about the meeting. I did. I checked my calendar the night before and said to myself, "I have that meeting in the morning." And when I got up that morning, I had absolutely no thought of that meeting whatsoever.

That's why I got an electronic brain, one of those handheld marvels of artificial intelligence that holds everything: addresses, phone numbers, task lists, journals, notes, books, calculators, games, e-mail, calendars, and appointments. I'd never miss another meeting. I'd never miss another anything. This would be my brain.

It seems the brain has a mind of its own. Lights blink. Alarms go off. It makes noises I'd never make in public. All the information I need is available at the touch of a button. But which button? I know this thing is brilliant. I just can't speak its language. And what good does it do me if I forget to take it with me? How often can I use the excuse, "I'm sorry. I left my brain at home"?

I had a high-tech problem. I discovered a low-tech solution: the Sticky Note System. The humble sticky note is a lifesaver for the middle aged. When I have an appointment, after writing it on my paper calendar and entering it in my electronic brain, I also write a reminder on several sticky notes. I stick one on the door leading out to the garage, another on the kitchen cupboard, a third on the bathroom mirror, and the last on my bedside lamp. This at least lowers the risk of missing another meeting.

The Sticky Note System is great, but not perfect. I keep a pad of stickies in the laundry room. On laundry day, I write "BUY SOAP" and stick the note to my shirt; later I stick it to the shopping list on the refrigerator. Unfortunately, by shopping day I'm wondering, *BUY SOAP? Was that dish, hand, dishwasher, bath, or dog soap?*

I keep sticky notes next to the TV so I can jot down good ideas from the "better living" channels. Later I look at the note stuck to the cupboard door and wonder, *Is this a recipe or instructions for home-made wallpaper paste?* I won't know until I taste it.

Sticky notes are handy in the car too. "PICK UP DRY CLEAN-ING" and "PICK UP HUSBAND" are good things to remember. (I chuckle at the irony as "GET GAS" flutters from the dashboard just as I pull into Taco Bob's drive-thru and order Bob's Bean Burrito Extremo Especiale, Extra Grande.)

Okay, so I'm losing it. The most encouraging research I've come across suggests that *mental* symptoms may be the first symptoms of the approaching "change of life." And these mental symptoms can start much earlier than you might think. In the forties. Even in the thirties! Yikes!

The list of possible mental symptoms is a long one. Reading the list, I thought, *Has this researcher been peeking in my windows?* "Bright" women (if it happens to "bright" women, what hope is there for the rest of us?) reported the following symptoms: losing their train of thought, forgetting what they'd just read, missing meetings, and misplacing things. *(Dogs, perhaps?)* At times, they felt cotton-headed and experienced foggy thinking. *(Hmm.)* They feared repeating themselves, asking, "Did I tell you this already?" *(Ha!)*

They had momentary lapses where they blanked out on an ingrained skill, such as how to start the car. They found themselves unable to focus and easily distracted. *(I had to read that part three times. Did you?)* They drew blanks trying to remember the words to songs, why they came into a room, birthdays, and ATM codes. *(Or kissing someone maybe?)*

Angry and frustrated, these bright women worried about the early onset of Alzheimer's, got depressed, and lost sleep. They had crying spells for no apparent reason. *(Gasp!)* They didn't want to admit these feelings for fear of eroding their own credibility and undermining others' confidence in them. *(Yes! Yes!)* They wanted to just give up trying, give up competing, and put themselves out to pasture like an old racehorse. *(Sob!)*

Been there. Felt that.

The really good news? These bright women were normal. NOR-MAL! These cognitive symptoms were the early warning signals of the physical changes to come. This "perimenopause" was a normal hormone-related condition, just as pregnancy is a normal hormone-related condition.

Given the size of the Baby Boom bulge in the population, I realized that millions of women out there were going through the same things I was experiencing. We were all together in the "pause" before menopause. And we weren't "losing it." We were all just being normal!

I informed my family. "Please, no more remarks about mentalpause or senior moments. I am simply exhibiting the symptoms accompanying normal hormonal changes. So I would appreciate it if you would stop implying — however subtle you think twirling your index finger next to your temple might be — that I am nuts!"

The following week, I knew they'd gotten my message. I had another momentary brain fade while I was talking to my daughter on the phone, and she said, "Well, Mom, you sure are normal today!" Yes!

It does help to lighten up. Just the other day, my husband and I discussed something important, about which I recall nothing now. I just know it was important! I told him, "It's that other shoe thing ..."

"What other shoe thing?" he asked.

"I feel like I'm waiting for the other shoe," I said.

"For the other shoe to ...?" I knew he was trying to help, but darned if I could remember what the "other shoe" was supposed to do. I did the only thing I could do. I laughed. "What's happening to me?" I wailed. "I'm losing it!"

"You're not the only one," he said. He looked around to make sure nobody else was listening. (We've been home alone for ages, but he still checks for "little pitchers.") He continued.

"Remember the other night you asked me to pick up milk on the way home? Well, I pulled into the garage and thought, *Oh, NO! I forgot the milk.* I reached into the backseat for my briefcase, and there on the floor in back were two gallons of milk. I hadn't forgotten to get it. I just forgot to remember that I got it!" I was glad the children weren't home to hear this.

Meanwhile, I'll rely on paper planners, my electronic brain, and the Sticky Note System. All of which will soon be obsolete, because medical science keeps promising to fix my brain. Each time I see an article about procedures or products that promise to reverse the effects of aging on the brain, hope flares briefly.

Can they do that? What if I am too far gone? What if my synapses are so soggy they can no longer fire? (My three remaining brain cells are packing at this point. I can feel it. I realize I'm hopeless. You have to give science something to work with.)

"The Lord giveth ..." and time taketh some of it away. That's just how it is. But omniscience has always been God's domain, not ours. What matters most, I see now, are not the brilliant flashes of insight I've had, but the quiet understandings I've come to.

It may take me twice as long now to think of half as much, but I'm not in such a hurry anymore. I enjoy taking extra time now to linger in God's love. "Abide with me," Jesus says. I long to rest in his fellowship, to know deeper peace in his presence. And the Holy Spirit is forever there, as promised in John 14:26, to help me remember what I've learned.

It may take me longer to put a name to a familiar face I see, but the day is coming when I will no longer "see but a poor reflection as in a mirror; then we shall see face to face. Now I know in part; then I shall know fully, even as I am fully known" (1 Corinthians 13:12). I will know Jesus when I see him, and as he promised, on that glorious day he will remember me.

He Could Have Just Said, "And Now, Ladies, Praise ..."
John Ortberg

ⓔ

There are people (I'm told) who genuinely don't like chocolate. There are tea drinkers who find the aroma of fresh-brewed Starbucks in the morning eminently resistible. But one hunger is universal. You have never met a person who doesn't long for more joy. W. H. Auden wrote, "Among those whom I like or admire, I can find no common denominator, but among those whom I love, I can: all of them make me laugh." More often than you can imagine, when people are stressed, worried, preoccupied, lonely, or afraid, they carry this sign just beneath the surface: "Joy needed — please lighten up."

The expression of authentic happiness is what researchers call a *zygomatic* smile. It takes its name from the zygomaticus muscles that produce it. The signs of a zygomatic smile are the lip corners turning upward and also crow's-feet showing around the eyes. Here is where the connection between the human body and the human spirit is truly amazing. We can show a polite grin or a camera smile at will. In such cases, people make their lips go up, but no crow's-feet are visible.

The polite smile can be manipulated; that is why the smiles that people put on their faces for photographs often look forced. But the zygomatic smile is hard to fake. It is a smile that goes all the way up to the eyes. The distinction begins early; five-month-old infants show the eye-muscle smile when the mother approaches, but a smile without the eye muscle when a stranger approaches.

People who don't take themselves too seriously give a great gift to those around them.

If you're willing to lighten up, even your mistakes can become bridges. The church where I work videotapes most of the services, so

I have hundreds of messages on tape. Only one of them gets shown repeatedly.

This video is a clip from the beginning of one of our services. A high school worship dance team had just brought the house down to get things started, and I was supposed to transition us into some high-energy worship by reading Psalm 150. This was a last-second decision, so I had to read it cold, but with great passion: "Praise the LORD! Praise God in his sanctuary; praise him in his mighty firmament!" The psalm consists of one command after another to praise, working its way through each instrument of the orchestra. My voice is building in a steady crescendo; by the end of the psalm I practically shout the final line, only mispronouncing one word slightly: "Let everything that has breasts praise the LORD."

A moment of silence. The same thought passes through four thousand brains: *Did he just say what I think he did? In church? Is this some exciting new translation I can get at the bookstore?*

Then everybody in the place just lost it. They laughed so hard for once I couldn't say a thing. It was zygomatic. I finally just walked off stage, and we went on with the next part of the service.

I have been teaching at that church for eight years. Of all the passages I have exegeted and all the messages I have preached, that is the moment that gets replayed before conferences and workshops. Over and over.

A Gentle Answer
Marsha Marks

A gentle answer turns away wrath, but a harsh word stirs up anger" (Proverbs 15:1). My husband, Tom, is the master of the gentle answer. Once when I was in a rage at him and I was out of town, I sent him an e-mail telling him that he was treating me like an idiot and I was furious about it. "I am not an idiot," I said, "and I won't be treated like one."

Within minutes of sending the e-mail, I called Tom on the phone and said, "Did you get my e-mail?"

He answered very gently, "Yes, but I have one question. What's an *eye-dot*?"

Apparently, I, who can't spell under the best of circumstances and really can't spell when I am angry, had spelled *idiot, i-d-o-t*. Repeatedly throughout the e-mail, I had written, "I am not an *idot* and I won't be treated like an *idot* and you are treating me like an *idot* and I won't stand for it."

I was laughing so hard at the end of Tom's reading back my e-mail to me that my anger was turned away. A gentle answer turns away wrath.

Living at Geriatric Junction
Barbara Johnson

*My bifocals are adequate, my dentures fit fine.
My face-lift is holding, but I sure miss my mind!*

We all know why God made it so difficult for women over fifty to have babies, don't we? Why, they would put them down someplace and forget where they left them! Of course, I only forget three things: names, faces, and … oh dear, I forgot the third!

Men are just as bad, I guess. They forget names and faces, not to mention birthdays and anniversaries. Later on they forget to pull their zippers up, and even later they forget to pull them down! If that isn't bad enough, think of their hair problems. The reason men don't need face-lifts is because sooner or later their face will grow right up through their hair. One man I talked to said when he was young he used to wash his hair with Head and Shoulders but now he uses Mop and Glow. A friend of mine who is completely bald refuses to wear turtlenecks, certain they would make him look like a roll-on deodorant! Here's a cure for baldness you might want to try: Mix one part Epsom salts with one part alum mixed with three tablespoons persimmon juice. Vigorously rub this mixture into your husband's scalp three times daily. It won't keep his hair from falling out, but it will shrink his head to fit the hair he has left!

One lady wrote about problems her husband was having as he grew older: "He's been doing dumb things," she said. "While I was away visiting my sister, he did the laundry by stuffing his dirty socks into water glasses, then putting them in the dishwasher. Then he wore the socks and drank out of the water glasses." (I warned this lady to stop visiting her sister and stick close to home.)

Another lady told me her husband just sat around with the remote in his hand. I comforted her with words I once heard some-one say: "If you love something, set it free. If it returns, you haven't lost it. If it disappears, it wasn't truly yours to begin with. If it sits there watching television, unaware it's been set free, you probably already married it!"

To women who worry about the passing years, I say, "Just relax and enjoy life, even the parts you can't remember!" After all, the only way to look younger is not to be born so soon! It's impossible to fool Mother Nature, no matter how much you exercise — especially when all you exercise is *caution*.

An old-timer, of course, is anyone who learned to ride a bicycle before it became a fitness machine. My middle-aged girlfriend started an aerobics program but quit because her thighs kept rubbing together and setting her pantyhose on fire! As for me, whenever I think about exercise, I lie down until the thought goes away. My idea of strenuous exercise is to fill the bathtub and lie back, then pull the plug and fight the current. How's that for maturity?

Nowadays most of us are a lot like ducks swimming in a lake — composed on the surface but paddling like crazy underneath. Real maturity, we discover, means being gentle with the young, compassionate with the elderly, and tolerant of the weak as well as the strong — because we have been all these things at one time or another. The best way to grow in maturity is to pray this little prayer every day: Thank you, dear God, for all you have given me, for all you have taken from me, for all you have left me!

I spoke recently at a retreat for "golden-agers," folks between seventy and eighty years old. Breakfast was to be served buffet style, with each table of ten going up for food. The table with the folks taking the most pills that morning would get to go first. That was the prize! With *seventy-two* pills (Bill and I had already taken ours in our room), our table took the honors.

As we grow older, pills and all, we need to carve out happiness and joy every day. But we can't do it by avoiding things. Trying to stave off age or trouble is like trying to nail Jell-O to a tree. We can only do it by entrusting more of ourselves to God each day.

One nice thing about the passing of years is that you and your children eventually wind up on the same side of the generation gap. You can avenge yourself on them by living long enough to cause them trouble. Another nice thing about aging is that each day you get closer to seeing the Lord. Imagine that scene! To me it has a silvery sheen; all sadness is transformed and everything dull will be made bright!

Reynolds Wrap celebrated its fiftieth anniversary last year. The salesman who sold the first roll of aluminum foil is still alive at age eighty-four. In fifty years Reynolds produced seventy-nine million miles of the stuff, enough to stretch from the earth to the moon and back 180 times! Something about that picture reminds me of God's silvery stuff stretching from heaven to earth many times over — wrapping us in his protective love as the years pass. Because of that I'm not afraid of aging, forgetfulness, pills, or creaky bones. I just remember that growing old is mandatory, but growing up is optional. I am always in my prime until I get wrinkles in my heart!

Prayers of a Passenger
Barbara Johnson

A lot of folks say they pray most fervently when they're riding with a bad driver! That reminds me of a story I heard about two little old ladies who were out for a drive in a large car. They were both so short their heads were barely visible above the dashboard.

As they were cruising along, they came to a red light, but they just went right on through it. Soon they approached another intersection, and the light there was also red, but the car didn't stop. After the car rolled through a third red light, the old woman in the passenger's seat shrieked to high heaven: "Mildred! Did you know you just ran through three red lights? You could have killed us!"

"Oh my stars!" Mildred exclaimed. "Am I driving?"

6

It's All in How You Look at It
(and Laugh at It)

*I'm not offended by all the dumb blonde jokes, because I know
I'm not dumb and I'm also not blonde.*

— Dolly Parton

Every time I close the door on reality, it comes through the windows.

— Jennifer Unlimited

Deception in the Perception
Gwendolyn Mitchell Diaz

B ack in the days when our local airport ran commuter flights to Tampa and Orlando, my husband often took the Friday afternoon flight out of town on his way to a speaking engagement. Dropping him off became almost a weekly family event. All four children, plus their strollers and toys, would pile into the station wagon with Mom and Dad, and we would head to the airport. We dropped Dad at the lobby door, then parked at the far end of the parking lot where we could watch his plane take off. While we waited, we played with our footballs and Frisbees and had a little snack. (We never knew quite how long he would be delayed, but we were prepared!)

As the plane roared down the runway, the kids climbed on top of the station wagon and waved and yelled "good-bye" to Dad — all except our three-year-old. He was always very involved in the activity up until that point; but suddenly, as the plane took off, he turned into a quiet little statue. Instead of waving and carrying on like the rest of us, he just stood on the ground quietly staring at the departing plane. With glazed eyes he gazed into the horizon watching the speck become smaller and smaller until it completely disappeared. I had to bodily pick him up and place him in his car seat for the ride home. Once we pulled into the driveway, his true, wild nature returned almost as abruptly as it had disappeared.

Again there would be a total change in his demeanor when we received a call from the airport and rushed off to pick up Dad on Sunday evening. Like a silent zombie, he would stare at his dad as he exited the lobby. "You're big!" he once exclaimed as his dad tossed him in the air. We laughed and agreed, "Yeah, Dad is pretty big!"

Then came the special day when we all got to go to the big airport in Tampa, get on an airplane with Dad, and fly to a conference in Texas. Everyone was excited — except our three-year-old.

He asked strange questions while we packed our suitcases. "Will my clothes still fit me when I'm in the airplane?" and "Does it hurt to be little?"

He walked like a zombie on the way to the airport, never uttering a word. He silently held my hand and tiptoed beside me as we made our way to the gate. Finally, it was time to get on board. There was pure excitement as we headed down the tunnel to the plane — except for child number three. His eyes were wide, and his lips were shut tight. We jockeyed for the best seats, got out the least noisy toys, and buckled up for takeoff.

"Here we go!" one of the boys shrieked as we headed down the runway. Silence from our three-year-old. "Look, we're in the clouds!" Another child was ecstatic. Not a peep from child number three. "Go, go, go!" yelled the baby. Our three-year-old sat as still as a stone.

Finally, he reached over and pulled my sleeve. In a small, shaky voice, he asked, "Mommy, when do we get real little?"

Seeing my puzzled expression, he tried to explain. "You know, like Daddy does when he gets on an airplane and it goes in the sky. He gets real little! When does that happen to us?"

Suddenly I understood his whole airport dilemma. He had absolutely no concept of depth perception — at least when it came to airplanes taking off. He had seen them shrink before his very eyes, diminishing everything within them, including Dad. He obviously concluded that he was about to be reduced to the size of a mosquito!

It took a lot of explaining, but finally he seemed to comprehend. He decided that airplanes were really cool after all. Several times I had to quiet him down on the trip as he laughed and played with his brothers.

I realized then that reality is not always as we perceive it, even when we see it with our very own eyes! Only God can see the total picture in all its proper dimensions.

Let's Face It
Marilyn Meberg

When Ken and I first moved to Laguna Beach, California, I was excited about walking the beach each morning as my exercise routine. I saw it as an exhilarating way to stay fit, to talk to the Lord, and to revel in my surroundings.

One morning, about three weeks into my daily reveling, I was making my way down to Main Beach when I noticed over my right shoulder what looked like a Doberman trotting some distance behind me. I had no reason to be alarmed, but I was the only one on the beach, and the dog was not on a leash. That made me a tad nervous. After all, Dobermans are known to be fierce guard dogs. Maybe he felt the need to fiercely guard the beach. I picked up my pace. So did he!

Looking edgily over my shoulder, I noticed the dog was gaining on me. He wasn't running, but he was doing what I'd call a fast trot. I too broke into a fast trot. That seemed to encourage him to increase his speed, so I increased mine. Within a short time, I was moving at a full-out run. So was he. I began to huff and puff. As the dog continued to gain on me, I envisioned newspaper headlines: "Middle-Aged Woman with Nostrils Full of Sand Found Facedown, Dead from a Massive Heart Attack." Or "Woman's Shredded Remains Found Scattered along the Sands of Laguna Beach, Unidentified Dog Sitting Close By with Blue Sweatshirt Threads Dangling from Mouth."

I didn't like either of those headlines, yet I knew within moments he would be upon me. So I abruptly stopped running and turned to face him. He was delighted. He came bounding up to me, tail wagging and obviously eager to be petted. I stroked his face and neck and then dropped onto the sand with exhaustion and relief. To his obvious delight I scratched his ears and told him what a fright he had given me. He didn't seem to comprehend anything other than that he had made a new friend. Together then, we ultimately arrived at Main Beach, with his stopping repeatedly to wait for me.

I have metaphorically applied that story to my life many times. For instance, I have envisioned certain fears that I would try to keep ahead of, only to find that when I stopped and faced them, there really was nothing to fear after all. What I needed to do was quit trying to avoid them and face them instead.

After my husband died, I didn't think I could handle money matters like taxes, interest rates, and investments. After all, I have a number phobia. No one with a number phobia can figure out and keep track of stuff more complex than the price of broccoli, cauliflower, and grapefruit. I had no choice but to turn and face that fear. I would still rather deal with investments like broccoli, cauliflower, and grapefruit, but I have learned it won't leave me dead on the beach to read a tax form.

Dashing ahead of the Dobermans of life leaves me breathless and scared. Facing them with a prayer on my lips and faith in my heart allows me not only to trust God more but also to experience victory that comes from no one but him. Actually, that is a rather exhilarating way to stay fit.

Don't Push the Button
Patsy Clairmont

◉

It all started when I named a file in my computer "Patsy." I realize that was a little vain, but I had run out of creative titles for my endless documents. When I finished with the file, I wanted to toss it out, which required a simple press of a button. But that's when the plot thickened. I told my machine to erase the file, and it inquired, "Are you sure you want to send Patsy to the recycle bin?"

Some days I'd yell, "Yes, send the old girl to the bin; she's getting on my last nerve!" But this wasn't one of those moments, and I found it difficult to push the button that would blast "Patsy" to smithereens — or wherever computers ship their discards.

Had the machine asked, "Are you sure you want to send Patsy to the spa?" I'd have pushed that button. Or "Are you sure you want to send Patsy to see her grandson, Justin?" Trust me, I'd personally pack her bags. But the discarding permanency of the computer's question troubled me.

Then I remembered a story in the book of Jeremiah when the prophet visited a potter's house. The craftsman had made a pot that was marred, so he decided to remake it (not discard it) into a different pot that pleased him.

I'm marred; how about you? Any cracks in your pot?

I've learned that the pressure in our lives often becomes the reshaping technique God uses to make us more pleasing. And, good news, he doesn't discard his own. Ever.

Lord, in your faithful molding I place my hope forever. Amen.

Truck-Stop Rose
Chonda Pierce

Before my husband and I were married, I don't think anyone ever told him he was supposed to buy me an anniversary gift *every* year. But through seventeen years of marriage, that's just one of those things he's had to learn. Thank goodness we've always lived close to a 7-Eleven (or a truck stop), and they sell those funny cards close to the cash register. You know, the ones that read, "Happy anniversary to the one I love, and welcome to Tennessee!"

I've received a few of those over the years, along with some nail clippers that have a catcher on the side for the trimmings, sort of like a lawn mower; some collector spoons of the states of Alabama and Arkansas; and a whole case of 10W-40 motor oil.

But the greatest gift came the year I received a dusty rose that really wasn't a rose at all.

Since our anniversary is in May, every now and then it falls close to Mother's Day. One year it fell on Mother's Day, and I knew right then I was going to get gypped — I always do on those two-for-one holidays. As we scrambled to pull ourselves and the children together for church, my husband suddenly froze up, turned white, and said, "Why don't you and the children head on to church, and I'll meet you there."

"Need to make a stop?" I knew right away what had happened — or in this case, had not happened.

He nodded, but not a big nod, somehow believing he would give away the "surprise" with a big nod.

The children and I headed on to church, stopping for doughnuts along the way, which gave David enough time to do his shopping and still arrive before me. He was standing in the foyer when we walked in, obviously holding something behind his back.

"Hi, honey." His face was about to break into a giant smile. Then he quickly pulled from behind him a silky-dusty-gray rose. "Happy anniversary *and* happy Mother's Day," he said. (Told you.)

I took the rose from him and thanked him while studying the flower. Something looked odd here, something besides the dust.

"It's a rose," he said.

"Yes."

"For Mother's Day."

"Yes."

"*And* our anniversary."

(Gypped.) "Yes."

Once I brushed away some of the dust, the flower didn't look nearly as gray. It looked almost white. I could even see the detail in the lace that edged some of the petals. One of the petals was more crooked than the others, so I gave it a little tug, and just like that the whole rose sprung open and dangled there before me like a broken Slinky. It took me only a couple of seconds before I realized that the rose wasn't a rose at all — it was underwear! And I'm not talking about the Fruit of the Loom kind either. This was more like dental floss! My mouth dropped open, David turned whiter than the rose — I mean, underwear — and Zach, who was six then, called out, "Go, Dad!" right there in the church foyer!

I hid the ... the ... *thing* behind my back just as some of our church friends walked by.

"Good morning, Margaret," I said, waving with my Bible.

"Good morning, Chonda," said Margaret. "My, you look like you got some sun this weekend."

Now I was fanning myself with my Bible. "Oh, yeah, I'm feeling just a little flushed."

I shoved stem and all into my purse, and somehow we shuffled on into the sanctuary. I think David and I were content to put this little incident behind us. Then the preacher called the ushers forward and announced to the congregation that because it was Mother's Day, he wanted to make sure every mother there received her special flower.

Uh-oh.

The ushers had baskets filled with red and white carnations, and the men moved along the aisles, passing out the fresh flowers. David took a single carnation from the basket and handed it to me, just as he had with the fake flower earlier. Everything seemed to be okay. It looked as if we were going to get out of this whole mess without any major embarrassment. That is, until Zach called from the far end of the row, "Hey, Dad, do you think that one will turn into underwear too?"

I learned that day that looks can be so deceiving. I know that's one of those real simple lessons you learn when you're two and the pretty bumblebee makes you cry. But sometimes those simple lessons need to be reviewed. I don't think there's any better way to be reminded than by unwrapping a pair of underwear in the church foyer. Yup, appearances can be very deceiving.

Plane Perception
Dan Clark

I was flying from San Francisco to Los Angeles. By the time we took off, there had been a forty-five-minute delay and everybody onboard was ticked. Unexpectedly, we stopped in Sacramento on the way. The flight attendant explained that there would be another forty-five-minute delay, and if we wanted to get off the aircraft, we would reboard in thirty minutes.

Everybody got off the plane except one gentleman who was blind. I noticed him as I walked by and could tell he had flown before because his seeing eye dog lay quietly underneath the seats in front of him throughout the entire flight. I could also tell he had flown this very flight before because the pilot approached him and, calling him by name, said, "Keith, we're here in Sacramento for almost an hour. Would you like to get off and stretch your legs?" Keith replied, "No thanks, but maybe my dog would like to stretch his legs."

Picture this: All the people in the gate area came to a completely quiet standstill when they looked up and saw the pilot walk off the plane with the seeing eye dog! The pilot was even wearing sunglasses. People scattered. They not only tried to change planes; they also were trying to change airlines!

If You're Happy and You Know It…

Barbara Johnson

Singing lifts our spirits — even if we can't carry a tune in a bucket! I learned this fact when the Billy Graham Crusade came to our area a few years ago. Because I'd been to other crusades, I knew that volunteer choir members were guaranteed good seats, so I signed up right away. My husband Bill and I wanted to go together, so I signed him up too, even though he can't sing at all!

As gently as I could during our rehearsals, I suggested to Bill that he just mouth the words silently so our little secret wouldn't be discovered. After all, I pointed out to him, lip-synching is a common thing among big recording stars! All went well through the rehearsals, but when the crusade itself began, Bill got caught up in the joyful exuberance of the soul-stirring music, and he belted out the hymns for all he was worth.

Now, there were hundreds of talented singers in that huge, majestic choir, and I doubt that anyone would have known about Bill's ear-numbing renditions except for one little thing. He had carried a tiny little tape recorder in his shirt pocket to tape the program. So he recorded himself loudest of all, and believe me, under normal circumstances, it would not be something you'd want to listen to more than once! But Bill's voice was so joyful that night, I can't help but love listening to that tape, even if his singing was a mile off-key and sometimes you can't tell if he's singing or in pain.

Ghost Story
Anonymous

Ⓔ

A man was on the side of the road hitchhiking on a very dark night in a little town in northern Minnesota, in the middle of a storm. The night passed slowly and no cars went by. The storm was so strong he could hardly see a few feet ahead of him. Suddenly, he saw a car looming, ghostlike, out of the gloom. It slowly crept toward him and stopped.

Reflexively, the guy got into the car and closed the door, then realized that there was nobody behind the wheel. The car slowly started moving again. The guy was terrified and too scared to think of jumping out and running. The guy saw that the car was slowly approaching a sharp curve. The guy started to pray, begging for his life; he was sure the ghost car would go off the road and he would plunge to his death, when just before the curve, a hand appeared through the window and turned the steering wheel, guiding the car safely around the bend. Paralyzed with terror, the guy watched the hand reappear every time they reached a curve. Finally, the guy gathered his wits and leaped from the car and ran to the nearest town.

Wet and in shock, he went into a bar and with his voice quivering ordered two shots of whiskey and told everyone about his horrible, supernatural experience. A silence enveloped everybody when they realized the guy was apparently sane and not drunk.

About half an hour later, Ole and Lena walked into the same bar. Ole says to Lena, "Look, Lena, dat's the guy dat rode in our car ven ve vas pushin' it in the rain."

7

Kid Stuff

Wrinkles are hereditary. Parents get them from their children.

— Anonymous

I have found the best way to give advice to your children is to find out what they want and then advise them to do it.

— Harry S. Truman

*It had been a long day with my five-year-old son,
a constant battle of wills which left both of us drained.
That night after he said his prayers and I had tucked him in,
he gave me a big hug, paused a moment, then whispered,
"Mommy, I love you more than I think I do."*

— Susan W.

*A confirmation student was asked to list the Ten Commandments
in any order. He wrote, "3, 6, 1, 8, 4, 5, 9, 2, 10, 7."*

— Anonymous

The Toddler's Diet
Anonymous

Over the years you may have noticed that most two-year-olds are trim. It came to me one day over a cup of grapefruit juice and a carrot that perhaps their diet is the reason.

After consultation with pediatricians, X-ray technicians, and distraught mothers, I was able to formulate this new diet. It is inexpensive and offers great variety and sufficient quantity. ENJOY!

Day 1:

Breakfast — One scrambled egg, one piece of toast with grape jelly. Eat two bites of egg using your fingers; dump the rest on the floor. Take one bite of toast, then smear the jelly over your face and clothes.

Lunch — Four crayons (any color), a handful of potato chips, and a glass of milk — three sips, then spill the rest.

Dinner — A dry stick, two pennies, four sips of flat diet pop.

Bedtime snack — Toast a piece of bread, butter it, and toss it facedown on the floor.

Day 2:

Breakfast — Pick up stale toast from the floor and eat it. Drink 1/2 bottle of vanilla extract or one vial of vegetable dye.

Lunch — Half tube of "Pulsating Pink" lipstick and one ice cube, if desired.

Afternoon snack — Lick an all-day sucker until sticky, take it outside, and drop in dirt. Retrieve and continue slurping until clean again, then bring inside and drop on living room carpet.

Dinner — A rock or an uncooked bean, which should be thrust up your left nostril. Pour iced tea over mashed potatoes, eat with spoon.

Day 3:

Breakfast — Two pancakes with plenty of syrup, eat with fingers, rub fingers in hair to clean. Glass of milk, drink half, stuff excess pancakes in glass. After breakfast, pick up yesterday's sucker from carpet, lick off fuzz until sticky again, then leave on cushion of your best chair.

Lunch — Peanut butter and jelly sandwich. Spit several well-chewed bites onto the floor. Pour glass of milk onto table, then slurp up.

Dinner — Dish of ice cream, handful of potato chips, one sip of cold coffee.

Final Day:

Breakfast — 1/4 tube of toothpaste (any flavor), bite of soap, one olive. Pour glass of milk over bowl of cornflakes, add 1/2 cup of sugar. Wait until cereal is soggy, drink milk, and feed cereal to dog with your spoon.

Lunch — Eat crumbs off the kitchen floor and dining room carpet. Find that sucker and finish eating it.

Dinner — A plate of spaghetti and chocolate milk. Leave meatball on plate. Take handful of cheese snacks, eat two, and place the rest in bowling ball holes or any other convenient hiding place.

Things I've Learned from My Children
Anonymous

ⓔ

- There is no such thing as child-proofing your house.

- If you spray hair spray on dust bunnies and run over them with roller blades, they can ignite.

- A four-year-old's voice is louder than two hundred adults in a crowded restaurant.

- If you hook a dog leash over a ceiling fan, the motor is not strong enough to rotate a forty-two-pound boy wearing underwear and a Superman cape. It is, however, strong enough to spread paint on all four walls of a twenty-by-thirty-foot room.

- Baseballs make marks on ceilings.

- You should not throw baseballs up when the ceiling fan is on.

- When using the ceiling fan as a bat, you have to throw the baseball up a few times before getting a hit.

- A ceiling fan can hit a baseball a long way.

- The glass in windows (even double-pane) does not stop a baseball hit by a ceiling fan.

- When you hear a toilet flush and the words "Uh-oh," it's already too late.

- Brake fluid mixed with Clorox makes smoke, and lots of it.

- A six-year-old boy can start a fire with a flint rock even though a thirty-six-year-old man says they can only do that in the movies.

- A magnifying glass can start a fire even on an overcast day.

- The fire department in San Diego has at least a five-minute response time.

- If you use a waterbed as home plate while wearing baseball shoes, it does not leak — it explodes.

- A king-size waterbed holds enough water to fill a two-thousand-square-foot house inches deep.

- Legos will pass through the digestive track of a four-year-old — Duplos will not.

- *Play-Doh* and *microwave* should never be used in the same sentence.

- Super glue is forever.

- No matter how much Jell-O you put in a swimming pool, you still can't walk on water.

- Pool filters do not like Jell-O.

- VCRs do not eject PB&J sandwiches even though TV commercials show they do.

- Garbage bags do not make good parachutes.

- Marbles in gas tanks make lots of noise when driving.

- You probably don't want to know what that smell is.

- Always look in the oven before you turn it on. Plastic toys do not like ovens.

- The spin cycle on the washing machine does not make earthworms dizzy. It will, however, make cats dizzy.

- Cats throw up twice their body weight when dizzy.

- Quiet does not necessarily mean don't worry.

- A good sense of humor will get you through most problems in life (unfortunately, mostly in retrospect).

Keeping Her Focus
Arnell Arntessoni

M y husband and I had been explaining the concept of childbirth to our five-year-old daughter, Michaela. I realized our conversations had hit home when she stuffed a doll under her shirt, making her tummy appear rather large. As she walked around the house groaning — obviously having "labor pains" — I asked her, "Are you going to have a baby soon?" She nodded and answered, "Yes, I'm already having distractions!"

Alterations
Hester Jones

Since my five-year-old son Jeff had a speaking part in our church's Easter program, I decided to buy him his first suit. We left it at the store to be altered.

When my husband came home that night, Jeff was bubbling over with excitement about his new outfit. When my husband asked to see it, Jeff said it was being "ordained."

"No, dear," I corrected him, "it had to be altered."

"That's right," Jeff replied. "I knew it had something to do with church."

When Laughter Stings
Mark Twain

As a boy, Samuel Clemens (Mark Twain) loved playing practical jokes. One of his favorite targets was a boy by the name of Jim Wolf, who lived with the Clemens family.

One afternoon I found the upper part of the window in Jim's bedroom thickly cushioned with wasps. Jim always slept on the side of his bed that was against the window. I had what seemed to me a happy inspiration: I turned back the bedclothes and, at cost of one or two stings, brushed the wasps down and collected a few hundred of them on the sheet on that side of the bed, then turned the covers over them and made prisoners of them. I made a deep crease down the center of the bed to protect the front side from invasion by them, and then at night I offered to sleep with Jim. He was willing.

I made it a point to be in bed first to see if my side of it was still a safe place to rest in. It was. None of the wasps had passed the frontier. As soon as Jim was ready for bed I blew out the candle and let him climb in in the dark. He was talking as usual but I couldn't answer, because by anticipation I was suffocating with laughter, and although I gagged myself with a hatful of the sheet, I was on the point of exploding all the time. Jim stretched himself out comfortably, still pleasantly chatting; then his talk began to break and become disjointed; separations intervened between his words and each separation was emphasized by a more or less sudden and violent twitch of his body, and I knew that the immigrants were getting in their work. I knew I ought to evince some sympathy, and ask what was the matter, but I couldn't do it because I should laugh if I tried. Presently he stopped talking altogether — that is, on the subject which he had been pursuing, and he said, "There is something in this bed."

I knew it but held my peace.

He said, "There's thousands of them."

Then he said he was going to find out what it was. He reached down and began to explore. The wasps resented this intrusion and began to stab him all over and everywhere. Then he said he had captured one of them and asked me to strike a light. I did it, and when he climbed out of bed his shirt was black with half-crushed wasps dangling by one hind leg, and in his two hands he held a dozen prisoners that were stinging and stabbing him with energy, but his grit was good and he held them fast. By the light of the candle he identified them, and said, "Wasps!"

It was his last remark for the night. He added nothing to it. In silence he uncovered his side of the bed and, dozen by dozen, he removed the wasps to the floor and beat them to a pulp with the bootjack, with earnest and vindictive satisfaction, while I shook the bed with mute laughter — laughter which was not at all a pleasure to me, for I had the sense that his silence was ominous. The work of extermination being finally completed, he blew out the light and returned to bed and seemed to compose himself to sleep — in fact he did lie stiller than anybody else could have done in the circumstances.

I remained awake as long as I could and did what I could to keep my laughter from shaking the bed and provoking suspicion, but even my fears could not keep me awake forever and I finally fell asleep and presently woke again — under persuasion of circumstances. Jim was kneeling on my breast and pounding me in the face with both fists. It hurt — but he was knocking all the restraints of my laughter loose; I could not contain it any longer and I laughed until all my body was exhausted, and my face, as I believed, battered to a pulp.

Jim never afterward referred to that episode and I had better judgment than to do it myself, for he was a third longer than I was, although not any wider.

I played many practical jokes upon him but they were all cruel and all barren of wit. Any brainless swindler could have invented them. When a person of mature age perpetrates a practical joke it is fair evidence, I think, that he is weak in the head and hasn't enough heart to signify.

Are We There Yet?
Martha Bolton

Each year you know it's coming. You try to prepare for it. You try to brace yourself for it. But no matter what you do, it seems you're never quite ready for ... the family vacation.

Family vacations, though, do have their plus side. They give you time to get to know one another again, time to communicate. I know whenever our family goes on vacation, the communication begins the moment we pull out of the driveway. My husband is usually the first to open up.

"Uh, dear," he'll begin, "why are we towing a six-foot U-Haul trailer full of suitcases when we're only going to be staying *four* days?"

"You're absolutely right, dear. I really should have rented the truck."

"But the only things you left behind were the carpets."

"That's not true," I'll answer. "What do you think I used for padding?"

The communication takes a different turn a few minutes down the road.

"Sweetheart," he says with a smile, "did you remember to turn off the sprinklers?"

"You never told me to turn off the sprinklers."

"Well, did you check to see if all the burners were turned off?"

"No, but don't worry. If the house catches fire, the sprinklers will put it out."

For some reason, that's never a good enough answer, and inevitably he'll announce, "I'm turning around. We're going back to check."

"Going back?" the kids grumble from the rear seat. "But, Dad, the neighbors will call the fire department if they see smoke coming out of our windows."

"Not necessarily. They'll probably just think your mother's cooking again."

And so we go back. We always go back. In fact, my youngest son once wrote a school paper on "How I Spent My Summer Vacation Making U-Turns in Front of My House."

After a quick recheck of the homestead, we continue on our trip and the communication resumes. It's the children's turn now to share their innermost feelings.

"Aren't we there yet?"

"Aw, man, when are we going to get there?"

"He's kicking me!"

"Am not!"

"Are too!"

"Dad, what does it mean when a policeman turns his red lights on behind you?"

This openness continues throughout the remainder of the trip.

"How come he always gets to sit by the window?"

"Can you turn the radio up louder? I still have some of my hearing left."

"What do you mean, the Grand Canyon doesn't have a roller coaster?"

Amazingly enough, though, by the time a family vacation is over, we really have grown a little closer. My husband and I can truthfully say we opened up more to the children — his wallet, my purse, our credit card holders. And the children haven't held back sharing their aspirations, their goals, like, "Now can we go home?"

Yes, a family vacation can be a wonderful thing. Just make sure you schedule a second vacation to rest up from it.

Labor Intensive
Shirley Clutter

As my grown daughter and I chatted one day at my home, she noticed her children were playing a bit too quietly. Upon investigation, she found that the kids had written with pen on a little plastic chair. She promptly sent them outside to clean it off. Sympathetic, I sprinkled some Comet on the chair. Apparently it worked, because moments later, five-year-old Tanner shouted, "Grandma, we need some more of that vomit!"

It's Been an Even Busier Week Than *He* Thought
Stella Ward Whitlock

Throughout the sermon, our three-year-old son, David, sat unusually still, listening enthralled to the stories of David and Goliath, David and Jonathan, David and his mighty victories in battle.

During a dramatic pause in the sermon, David's awestruck stage whisper carried throughout the sanctuary as he asked my husband, "Daddy, when did I do all that?"

Side by Side
Sharon K.

I was sitting down to read a book to my three children, and they all wanted to sit next to me. Finally, I said, "Mommy only has two sides, so only two of you can sit next to me at a time. We'll have to take turns."

My youngest, who was almost three, promptly said, "Mommy, let's pray right now and ask Jesus to send us another side so that there will be enough sides for all of us."

Church Kids
Various Authors

A friend who teaches Sunday school told me about a time when she asked a question of some of the young children in her class. "What do you have to be to get into heaven?" she said.

One little boy shyly raised his hand and said softly, "Dead?"

— Tom R. Kovach

When a new child visited our Sunday school, the teacher greeted him and asked his age. The little boy held up four fingers.

"Oh, you're four," said the teacher. "And when will you be five?"

The child stared at her and after a few seconds replied, "When I hold up the other finger."

— Florence C. Blake

Our family had just joined a new church. My husband has trouble remembering names, so he often called our new minister "the preacher." We were relaxing at home one afternoon when the doorbell rang. Our four-year-old daughter, Molly, ran to get the door.

"Who is it?" I called out from the kitchen.

"It's the creature!" she exclaimed.

"What?" I said, heading for the living room.

"The creature," she shouted. "It's the creature that lives at church!"

Our red-faced pastor stood on the threshold. "I've been called a lot of things, but this tops them all," he chuckled.

— Emily M. Akin

As the Christmas Eve congregation stood for prayer, a little girl in the pew ahead placed her doll on the seat beside her. I looked down at the ugliest doll ever. It had a cartoon character face and a bulbous nose. A pink ribbon with an attached pacifier hung from its neck.

Impulsively, I put the pacifier into the doll's mouth to see if the girl would notice. After three quick clicking noises, the doll emitted a high-pitched, nonstop wail.

Everyone stared, and the mother glared at her daughter. "I told you not to put that pacifier in during church!"

"But, Mom, I didn't," the little girl said.

"It's my fault. I did it," I confessed. My face burned, rivaling the brightest poinsettia.

The mother turned and gave me an equally sharp glare.

"I'm so sorry. I didn't realize her doll would make noise."

After the prayer, we all returned to our seats. And just as my face was returning to a normal color, by husband stage-whispered over the heads of our giggling teenage daughters, "Honey, I would've gotten you your own doll for Christmas if you'd have asked."

— Connie Pettersen

I was trying to impress upon my first-grade Sunday school class the importance of individually receiving God's gift of salvation. I thought a simple illustration might be helpful. "What do you do when someone gives you a birthday present?" I asked.

One little girl was quick to answer: "You say, 'Thank you' — unless it's clothes. Then you put a really sad look on your face."

— Jo Ann Cook

8

Dad's a Hoot!

*I've wanted to run away from home more often
since I've had kids than when I was a boy.*

— Anonymous

A father is a banker provided by nature.

— French proverb

Laughing Matters
Phil Callaway

On Sunday afternoon I usually manage to make it to the couch shortly after the dishes are done, but today I didn't quite make it. Today I hit the floor in the living room and drifted off to sleep within seconds. My children saw me there, a rather large and inviting target, I suppose, because the three of them pounced upon me as I slept. I'm sure it was funny for them, but I happened to be dreaming at the time. In my dream two KGB officers, who suspected me of concealing military secrets in my trench coat, were pursuing me on foot through the darkened back alleys of our small town. They cornered me by a garden shed, pinning me by the arms. I tried to wiggle. I could not. Waking, I found a child sitting on one of those arms, another on the other, and the third on his way to the pantry to get a Cheerio. Pulling my shirt up, he inserted the piece of cereal in my belly button. "Here, Mojo!" he yelled, and the dog came running.

Pointing to the Cheerio, he hollered, "Get it, get it, get it!"

You have choices at such a time. Not many of them. But there are a few. I chose to join in. "Whatever you do," I said, between gasps of painful laughter, "don't put honey on my forehead."

You know what happened next.

They even dabbed it on my lips. Children make us cry sometimes, but more often they help us laugh.

My son Jeffrey has a contagious laugh, one that spills out of his room, down the street, and even into the church. When he was very small, he started screaming during a sermon, so I grabbed him and whisked him out the back. As I pushed open the doors he yelled over my shoulder, "Pray for me!"

The Car of My Schemes
Dave Meurer

It was the kind of car most guys only dream about — a painstakingly restored 1957 Chevy Bel Air with an off-white top, a deep burgundy body, and a crushed velvet interior — and it had been delivered to *my* driveway earlier that day.

"It is beautiful," my wife agreed. "But not very practical."

"Practical, schmacktical!" I retorted, employing powerful logic to overcome her objection. "This is the quintessential American car! In Detroit people can legally *marry* this car! We'll just take a few commonsense precautions, like parking it in the garage at night, putting a cover on it in public parking lots, and hiring 'Vinnie the Enforcer' to follow it wherever it goes."

There was NO way we were getting rid of that car.

"There's one other thing," Dale said. "Mark just turned sixteen, which means he is going to be wanting to drive a *lot*, and I can just envision an absolute whining festival over who gets the keys. I don't think I can take all the sniveling and begging."

I smiled and nodded in the condescending "there, there" manner Dale has always found so endearing.

"I mean it," she warned. "Look me in the eyes and read just how serious I am. I do *not* want this car to turn into a source of conflict. You are going to have to be really tough."

"It won't be a problem," I assured her.

Fifteen minutes later ...

"Oh, please, please, please, please, *puh-leeeeeeease*? I promise I'll stick to back roads! It won't get a scratch. I won't eat while I drive! I just want to show it off to my friends! Please? C'mon! Please?"

Dale stormed into the room in the middle of the beg-a-thon.

"Is this about what I *think* it is about?" she demanded.

Mark cast a desperate, pleading look at her. "Mom, Dad is whining about my car again! I thought you had a talk with him."

"Oh, pleeeeeeeeeeeeeeeeease," I said again, falling to my knees and clutching his ankles. "Just let me take it around the block!"

"I told you already! You need to show some maturity first!" Mark replied firmly.

"Oh, *that's* a good one," Dale said dryly.

"But I didn't mean to rev the engine at the traffic light," I whimpered. "The gas pedal got stuck! It wasn't my fault that the guy next to us thought I wanted to race!"

Dale's jaw tightened as she looked at me.

"Tell me, was it the 'no sniveling' or the 'no begging' part that was confusing?" she asked in that slow, measured tone that means the addressee should forward himself to another room.

It just wasn't fair!

My father had called me a week earlier to explain that he wanted Mark to have the '57, which had been in the Meurer family for more than two decades.

"Why can't you give it to ME?" I wailed. "I'm your own flesh and blood SON! Mark is a distant relative at best — a virtual STRANGER! In fact, I have always suspected he was accidentally switched with another baby at the hospital. Don't compound the tragedy by signing the '57 over to this shameless IMPOSTOR."

"It isn't a gift, Son. I am going to let my *grandson* buy it from me," Dad explained. "He needs a good deal on some wheels now that he is sixteen. Besides, I think it will help him mature. It will teach him responsibility."

"But I need to mature, too! And I still need to learn responsibility! Just ask Dale," I cried.

"I think it is too late for you," Dad said. "But I still have hope for your kids."

This horrible situation was made all the more horrible by the fact that all my life I have had a series of ugly, loser cars that broke down at every opportunity and made no secret of the fact that they hated me. I have owned a 1969 Volkswagen hatchback, which is *not* to be confused with those charming little VW bugs we all know and love. No, the hatchback would have been better named the "hunchback." Pedestrians would literally clutch their ears and start yelling, "The bells!!! The bells!!!" when I drove by.

Then I had a 1977 AMC Pacer, which was voted "Ugliest Car of the Year" by *Motor Trend* magazine. The Pacer looked like you took a Ford Pinto and *inflated* it until the windows bulged out like toad eyes.

I had other even WORSE cars, which I am so embarrassed about that I will not even mention them other than to note that when someone crashed into one of them and totaled it, Dale began jumping up and down singing, "Ding-dong! The witch is dead!"

I *deserved* to finally drive a cool car to make up for all my prior humiliation!

I tried negotiating a deal with Mark, but he was a brutally tough bargainer.

"Mark, I'll paint flames on the sides of the station wagon; think how much more storage space you'll have than in the Chevy! It will be a straight-across trade. You don't have to give me a dime, and I'll even throw in one of those air fresheners that look like a little cardboard pine tree."

"How tempting," he mused. "Maybe you could also offer to let me walk on hot coals or fling myself off the dam."

"Sure! It would be sort of like a big waterslide! And it would probably feel refreshing after those coals!" I replied.

Needless to say, I am still driving my aged wagon, and Mark has one of the coolest cars in town.

To add insult to injury, Dale won't even ride with me in the station wagon since I had those flames painted on the fenders.

While You Were Away
Anonymous

Several years ago, I returned home from a trip just when a storm hit, with crashing thunder and severe lightning. As I came into my bedroom about 2:00 a.m., I found my two children in bed with my wife, Karen, apparently scared by the loud storm. I resigned myself to sleeping in the guest bedroom that night.

The next day, I talked to the children and explained that it was okay to sleep with Mom when the storm was bad, but when I was expected home, please don't sleep with Mom that night. They said okay.

After my next trip several weeks later, Karen and the children picked me up in the terminal at the appointed time. Since the plane was late, everyone had come into the terminal to wait for my plane's arrival, along with hundreds of other folks waiting for their arriving passengers. As I entered the waiting area, my four-year-old son saw me and came running, shouting, "Hi, Dad! I've got some good news!"

As I waved back, I said loudly, "What is the good news?"

"The good news is that nobody slept with Mommy while you were away this time!" Alex shouted.

The airport became very quiet, as everyone in the waiting area looked at Alex, then turned to me, and then searched the rest of the area to see if they could figure out exactly who his mom was.

Alien Impostor Boys
Dave Meurer

During my entire childhood it seemed like my mom was perpetually astonished by the fact that I was growing up. I would walk into the house after kindergarten — or third grade, or high school — and she would, on a regular basis, stare at me wide-eyed and say something like, "I just can't believe how *tall* you are getting! It seems like just *yesterday* you were a toddler!"

And I would reply, "So what do you want me to do, shrink?"

And she would just shake her head and walk away, still making incredulous comments.

One day as a high school sophomore, I came into the house, and Mom was — once again — absolutely *shocked* by my appearance. She gaped at me and appeared ready to faint. You'd think I had grown a third nostril or something.

"Why, it seems like just yesterday you were eating paste in Mrs. Marshall's kindergarten class! What happened to you?" she exclaimed, shaking her head.

I was exasperated.

"Mom, you just saw me this morning! I haven't grown any observable amount today! What is so surprising?"

I could never understand why Mom would get all weepy and sentimental about a simple biological process. Living things grow. This is natural. Kids get bigger. So what?

But from the way she talked about it, you'd think someone had slipped her a Rip Van Winkle pill and she'd spent years at a time in a coma, awakening just often enough to be amazed at how much her children had changed since she dozed off during the Lyndon Johnson administration.

I, on the other hand, was champing at the bit to make time move even faster so I could get a driver's license and then graduate from high school and move on to college and be independent and start to really live my life. Time was already moving too slowly as far as I was concerned, but it almost seemed like Mom wanted the clock to stand still completely.

"You just won't understand until you have children of your own," Mom said.

I finally got to test her hypothesis when I married Dale and became the father of Mark and Brad. One day as I left for work, Mark was just starting to take his first tentative steps. He would crawl over to the couch, clutch the cushions with his tiny hands, pull himself up, and then take unsteady strides as he hugged the furniture for balance. Dale and I clapped and gave him encouragement, and I could hardly wait to get home so I could see his progress. Unlike my misty-eyed, hopelessly sentimental mom, I welcomed the advances of each new day as a normal part of the growth process.

I finally arrived home, eager to play our favorite game of "horsey ride," where I would bounce Mark on my leg while holding his hands. And I was really looking forward to seeing how his walking had improved in my absence.

I walked in the door and called out, "I'm home!"

Typically Mark would come crawling excitedly down the hall, leaving behind a trail of drool. But this time he *walked* right into the living room with no hesitation at all.

"Hi, Dad. Can you take me and Kyle to the mall?" he asked.

"AAIIIEEEEEEE!" I shrieked.

Mark jumped back in alarm.

"What's wrong?" he asked, concern etched in his Clearasil-laden brow.

"WHAT HAPPENED TO YOU?!" I shouted. "You were just barely starting to walk, and now you are a TEENAGER and you are asking for a ride to the MALL!!!"

Mark sighed. "Please, not that again. You and Mom have gotten so weird ever since I started driver's education."

"AAIIIEEEEEEE!" I shrieked again. "How long have I been in a coma? You can't be learning to drive! You're supposed to be a baby!!! We were supposed to play horsey ride!!"

"On second thought, I think I'll walk to the mall," Mark replied, edging toward the door.

"You aren't going ANYWHERE until you eat a jar of paste!" I barked, as I rummaged through my office.

But when I turned around, he was gone.

I ran down the hall to find Dale, but bumped into yet another teen boy who had the faint beginnings of a mustache.

"Hi, Dad. Can you sign the form for my high school electives courses for next year? I was thinking of taking Spanish."

"AAIIIEEEEEEE!" I howled, barreling down the hall.

"You prefer French, apparently," he called after me as I locked myself in our bedroom, where Dale was putting away some clothes.

"You need to brace yourself, hon," I said, gripping her hands in mine. "Something bizarre and unearthly has happened. Something right out of a science fiction movie. Something too strange to be true."

Dale looked at me intently, then said, "So you actually remembered to write down an ATM transaction?"

"This is no time for joking," I snapped. "We turned our backs for a moment, and our kids have been transformed into giants! They are supposed to be using crayons and riding tricycles, and instead they are taking driver's education courses and growing more body hair than KoKo the Gorilla! Something has happened to our little boys!"

"Well, they can't stay young forever," Dale replied, smiling.

"THEY DIDN'T STAY YOUNG FOR THREE MONTHS!" I shot back. "Something has gone horribly wrong! Maybe I have been a guinea pig in a secret government experiment! Or maybe our kids were abducted by aliens, and these are alien impostor boys!"

"I think someone needs a glass of warm milk and a nap," Dale replied.

She was clearly in denial, poor soul. So I did what any mature male would do when confronted by such a terrifying phenomenon. I called my mom.

"Mom, something weird and inexplicable has happened," I began. "Our kids have sprouted up overnight like beanstalks on steroids! It's unnatural! At the rate they're growing, within three weeks they'll make Michael Jordan look like one of the Seven Dwarves!"

"Well, I always said you would understand someday," she replied, laughing. "It happens so fast. This is just like when you were growing up."

"NO, IT ISN'T!" I cried. "I think they're ALIENS! Can't you see? Put it all together! Bizarre, unearthly growth patterns! And that unintelligible music they listen to! It's a secret alien code from the mother ship! Aliens have abducted our sweet little toddlers and replaced them with creatures from the planet Zitlot 5. They are eating us out of house and home, sucking up all the hot water for their abnormally long showers, and even making us pay for their basketball shoes! It is a huge interstellar scam, and we are the victims! I want my babies back! I want to play horsey and take them on piggyback rides and read *Green Eggs and Ham* and watch them battle the pediatrician!"

Mom let me finish my tirade before she spoke.

"Now you understand what I meant when I kept telling you how fast time was flying," she said. "But what I didn't know back then, and what I will share with you now, is that there actually is a way to turn back the clock and recapture those days. So don't panic. I'll let you in on the secret."

"Well?" I asked impatiently.

She paused.

"Grandchildren," she replied.

I can hardly wait. I just wish time could move faster ...

Like Father, Like Son
Reverend Ronald B. Hughes

Seven years ago, when my oldest son was six, he was sitting in our church service with his mother while I preached from the pulpit. My topic was parenting, and I was trying to make the point that we must not only talk God's truth but walk it.

I told the congregation that my favorite child-rearing proverb is "It doesn't matter what you say to your children; they will grow up to be just like you." After I made that statement, I confessed that it scared me. I then asked if it scared anyone else. I looked out over the congregation to see that the only person with his hand raised was my son.

What a Character!
Dave Meurer

T he boys need to be at school extra early tomorrow for that project," I mentioned casually to Dale one evening as we were getting into bed. "Plus, the weather report says we are going to have
a nasty storm first thing. Fortunately for you, I am going to be the
thoughtful and compassionate husband in the morning."

"Thanks, hon," she grinned.

"Don't mention it," I replied.

Unusually alert considering the lateness of the hour, Dale immediately noticed that the alarm clock had been moved to her side of
the bed.

"What is *this* doing here?" she asked suspiciously.

"Like I said, the kids have to go to school early," I replied.

"You just told me YOU were going to take them!" she retorted.

"No, I said I was going to be thoughtful and compassionate," I
corrected. "Part of being a good husband is doing what is in the best
interest of your spouse. I'm just trying to be helpful."

"I am completely confused," Dale replied. "Are you saying you
are or are *not* planning to take the kids to school?"

"Hon, I would love to drive the kids to school. But as husbands
and fathers, we men have a special obligation to the character development of our families. Like it or not, God has given us this role.
I think getting up early to take the kids will help develop your
character. I am willing to give up this valuable character-building
opportunity so that you can grow as a person," I explained.

"Oh, *now* I get it," she replied, slapping her hand on her forehead.
"This is all for *my* own good! And heaven knows *you* don't need any
character development! Why, you have more character in your left
ear than I have in my entire body! You are a walking festival of
character! A veritable character factory, belching excess virtue out
of your character smokestack!"

I blushed at the flattery.

"Well, I don't know if I'd go *quite* that far, but you are getting the general idea," I said.

"Oh, but I've only just begun!" she exclaimed. "You have so much surplus character that you could ship it to India and dole it out to underprivileged children! We could sell your superfluous character by the pound at huge discount warehouses! Soon the entire nation will be awash in all the extra character you have been wasting all these years!"

"Dale, if I didn't know you better, I would suspect you are getting a little bit sarcastic," I said suspiciously.

"Not at all," she replied. "Your extra character is the talk of the town. In fact, at church last week Pastor Paul came up to me and asked, 'How do you manage to *live* with that character?'"

"You know, I could take that two ways," I mused.

"You can figure out which way he meant it as you drive the kids to school tomorrow," she replied, handing me the alarm clock.

Some women are very resistant to character development.

Easy-to-Clobber
John Ortberg

When our children were small, there were three words I hated more than any others in the English language. Sometimes the phrase read, "Easy to assemble," but nothing ever was. Tab A never fit into slot B. One Christmas Eve we foolishly purchased three "easy-to-assemble" gifts. At about one in the morning, after two and a half hours of irritation and anger, I finally said to my wife, "Do you want some help with that?"

Too Many Questions
Brenda Nixon

It was a crisp autumn night in a crowded school auditorium, and I was scheduled to speak to an audience of elementary school parents on the topic of discipline. Prior to the start of the evening's event, the program planner and I were talking privately.

"We have a large group here tonight," she observed with a sparkle in her eye.

"It's gratifying to see so many parents wanting to learn about effective discipline," I replied.

"I hope we get to hear everything you want to say," she whispered. "Sometimes they start asking too many questions and get the speaker off track."

"Let's ask everyone to hold their questions until the end of the program," I suggested.

"Okay, that's a plan," she agreed.

Soon she stood at the podium to introduce me. Politely she announced, "We have so much material to cover tonight, I want to make sure Brenda has a chance to share it. So please hold all your questions until the end of her presentation." She stepped aside and signaled for me to take the floor. I stood at the podium and opened my mouth to begin. Instantly, one father waved his hand to indicate a question. Ignoring his gesture I shared my first point. After some awkward moments — me speaking over his relentless motioning — his wife yanked down his hand.

I ended my talk on children and discipline that evening. Then I opened the floor with, "Does anyone have questions?"

Immediately the same dad raised his hand. Looking at him in acknowledgment, I asked, "What is your challenge?"

"My son never listens to the rules!" he said.

9

Mom's Always Good for a Laugh

Some are kissing mothers and some are scolding mothers, but it is love just the same, and most mothers kiss and scold together.

— Pearl S. Buck

The real menace in dealing with a five-year-old is that in no time at all you begin to sound like a five-year-old.

— Jean Kerr

Pick Your Battles ...
Veeery Carefully
Julie Ann Barnhill

I detest cauliflower and asparagus and have never forced my children to eat either of them "because they're good for you." I have, however, engaged in a ferocious battle of wills with my second child over macaroni and cheese.

One evening this child insisted (whined, fussed, begged, pleaded) that I make him a special order of said pasta for supper. I did. This child then refused to eat it and requested (whined, fussed, begged, pleaded) another food item. Setting his dinner plate in front of him, I said, "No, you're going to eat this macaroni and cheese because you asked for macaroni and cheese. *Capiche?*"

He no understand.

I translated, "You'll sit here until you eat the macaroni." Four hours later I wrapped the macaroni with Cling Wrap, tucked the delinquent into bed, and whispered in his ear, "I guess you'll be having cold mac and cheese for breakfast, because one way or another you're going to eat what you asked for." Eight hours later he consumed said food item — then promptly threw up at the table.

I found out later that his school served macaroni and cheese for lunch that day. Is there an odd sense of justice in this world for mothers or what?

A Mother-Mortification Moment
Marti Attoun

ⓔ

*H*it track six," I told my son as soon as he fed his Fountains of Wayne CD into the car player. "I like that 'Valley Winter Song.'"

His sigh shook the little Toyota.

Here's what happened: My kids have imposed their music on the car's airspace and driver for so long that I've grown rather fond of some of their bands. If you're trapped together long enough, you'll bond with Godzilla.

Not that there's any comparison, of course, but you get the idea.

I've driven to the grocery store so many times with Beck, Guster, and my new best friends — Fountains of Wayne — keeping me company that I consider all of us buddies. I even like to sing (or rather, bray) along.

"Please, Mom. Don't even start ...," my fifteen-year-old pleaded when I cut loose while traveling down Main Street with my elbows dancing, torso twisting, and head bopping to "Stacy's Mom."

"Oh, don't worry," I told him. "Our windows are rolled up. No one can hear me."

"Someone might *see* you," he hissed.

"Someone" refers to that subspecies — fifteen-year-old girls — who might be riding nearby with their own elbow-bouncing mothers.

The louder I sang, the lower my son sank in the passenger seat. A few blocks later, he pulled the seat-release trigger and dropped into the backseat. I appeared to passersby to be singing and carrying on quite an animated conversation with the steering wheel.

This mother-mortification moment made me pause, though, because I had a flash of unsettling memory. In the 1970s, I walked into our house and caught my mother in the act of ironing to John

Denver. It stopped me cold in my four-pound hiking boots, which resembled my hero's as closely as I could get in Joplin, Missouri.

John Denver was my Fountains of Wayne. I wore plaid flannel shirts like John's, even in August. I blistered my fingertips until I mastered the three guitar chords required for "Leaving on a Jet Plane." I thumbtacked his posters to my bedroom walls.

My cousin Mary and I even stole away in my folks' Chevy en route to the Rocky Mountains until guilt and low fuel made us U-turn in the middle of Kansas.

It threw me off-key to discover that my own mother — for who knows how long — had been secretly cozying up to *my* music.

My reclining son mumbled something smart-alecky about how I should be listening to Lawrence Welk at my age. I didn't dare tell him that one melody could work its magic on two generations at once.

Later, I heard him relating the incident to his sister and talking about how Fountains was going to be on David Letterman.

"Ooh," I squealed. "When? We'll all have to watch it together."

They looked as though I'd asked them to dine on raw gizzard.

"Hey," I said, "maybe they'll have a concert nearby and we all can go. What do you think?"

Neither one answered, but I get the feeling that soon I'll be reclaiming my car's airspace and tuning in to my favorite NPR station without any back talk. And when no one else is listening, I may even pop in "Stacy's Mom."

Sprinkles of Grace
Carol Kuykendall

ꙮ

Before I became a mom, I imagined that mothering would bring out the best in me. I'd take charge and be in complete control of my time, my emotions, and my children. I'd make the right decisions and then simply carry them out. Head over heart. Mind over matter. After all, that's what moms are supposed to do.

What was I thinking?

After becoming a mom, of course I learned that I don't always do the right thing, even when I know what the right thing is. But I like to think that's when God sprinkles me and my children with his grace. Take this example.

Late one afternoon, while grocery shopping with both a toddler and a preschooler stuffed into my cart (the same two children who had been pushing me to my limits all day long), I totally lost my ability to think rationally. They were whining about being hungry. I was hungry. We were all tired. They wanted cookies. I have to admit, I wanted cookies too. More than cookies, I wanted peace. No whining.

"Please, Mommy, please, Mommy. Mommy! Cookies. We want cookies."

Everything in my head logically told me, *You don't give children cookies just because they whine for cookies. You don't give children cookies an hour before dinner. Saying "No!" to cookies builds character in children and teaches them about delayed gratification and reinforces the fact that you — the mother — are in control here.*

"Please, Mommy: I need a cookie! Cookie!" they said in unison, pointing to a package on the shelf in the long (*very* long) cookie aisle.

Something inside me snapped. I don't know exactly what. But I do remember grabbing the package of cookies off the shelf, ripping it open, and then handing some cookies to the two children in my cart. I even ate a couple myself.

It didn't make sense, but it made silence, and at that moment, I wanted silence more than sense, even though the decision went against everything I knew in my head.

Later I felt a twinge of guilt when the checker lifted the half-empty package of cookies out of my cart and grinned at my two cookie monsters who still had sticky crumbs smeared across their faces.

"It's okay," she said as she ran the package across her scanner. "I'm a mom too."

Though we were total strangers, she and I shared an intimate moment of understanding that moms sometimes do what works instead of what's right. As I wheeled my cart out of the store, filled with groceries and two contented children, I couldn't help but think that God understands these mom moments too, and cuts us some slack as he sprinkles us with his grace.

Heir-Conditioning
Barbara Johnson

Children aren't happy with nothing to ignore,
And that's what parents were created for.

Motherhood: If it were going to be easy, it never would have started with something called *labor*. Kids can certainly test your patience — and your sense of order too. In a last-ditch effort to save her home from total chaos, one mother resorted to putting little reminder notes all over her house.

Inside her refrigerator: "There is no known sea-green food. If noticed, please remove it before it walks away."

In the bedrooms: "Having to make your beds is not considered child abuse."

On the dryer: "Match every sock with something; color or pattern not important."

In the family room: "Items of clothing do not have wheels. They must be carried (to your closets)."

In the bathroom: "Flushing is an equal opportunity job; please press firmly on the lever."

On the tub: "Brand-new studies reveal that soap, when submerged in water, will dissolve!"

Parenting is relentless. We keep waiting for it to get easier, but it doesn't. If you are a parent afflicted with hardening of the attitudes, certain you're *always* right, you will identify with the mother who searched a Hallmark store for the "I told you so!" card section. If you've assumed the role of Grand Potentate over the years, it's time to abdicate. Ask yourself, *Will my being right actually change the course of history?* Take a giant leap and admit the obvious: It's wrong to always be right. Children do not care how much you know until they know how much you care.

When things are bad between you and your children, take comfort in the thought that things could be even worse. Believe me, I know! And when they *are* worse, find hope in the fact that things can only get better. This parenting business is tough. For stress relief now, take a little nap or a long walk. And keep your sense of humor handy — like a needle and thread, it will patch up so many things!

Kids are always learning, from everything you *aren't* trying to teach. They learn, for example, that after a kid stops believing in Santa Claus, a kid gets underwear for Christmas. Resist the temptation to argue. Listen to your kids and learn what's really on their minds.

Remember that patience is the ability to idle your motor when you feel like stripping your gears. Being a parent also means working without a net. Even if you're scared to death, you have to keep going, looking straight ahead and always looking up. Try to brighten *up* a room, polish *up* the silver, and lock *up* the house while your kids work *up* appetites, think *up* excuses, and stir *up* trouble. Before you had them, you believed the old saying that children brighten up a home. Now you know they do, because they never turn off the lights! There is nothing more secure for either parent or child than knowing and loving the heavenly Father above. Now that's a real picker-upper!

When you decided to become a mother, you gave your heart permission to forever walk around outside your body. When that little wiggling child was placed in your arms, you knew nothing would ever be the same again. As kids change and grow, come and go, just keep the hearth fires burning. And remember that mothers should be like quilts, keeping kids warm without smothering them.

For their part, kids are like sponges — they absorb all your strength and leave you limp, but give them a squeeze and you get it all back! And let's face it: Child rearing is a pretty cool job — the biggest "heir-conditioning" job ever!

Check, Please!
Marti Attoun

Daily, I see myself sinking deeper and deeper into my mother's footsteps. It's just a matter of time before I'm wearing a plastic rain bonnet even when it's sunshiny and storing my quarters in empty baking-powder cans.

One habit of my mother's, though, has yet to take hold. Mom has an uncanny ability and agility when it comes to snatching a restaurant tab — or any other bill, for that matter. She insists on paying her own way and then some.

Just last Sunday, my sister hauled a takeout chicken dinner to Mom's for several of us to munch on.

"Where's the receipt?" Mom demanded before she even looked at the drumsticks. "I'm paying for that chicken."

"No, Mom," my sister shouted back. "This was my idea today, and I'm paying!"

While my sister peeled the lids from the green beans and mashed potatoes, Mom pounced on the empty bag and gleefully extracted the greasy receipt. She counted down to the penny the price of the meal, then crammed the wad of cash and coins into my sister's purse and zipped it with a vengeance.

"Well, I think it's ridiculous that you always insist on paying," my sister said.

Mom sniffed. "I'm no freeloader. If I'm not paying, then I'm not eating," she said. "I ought to be able to do something nice for someone once in a while."

I can assure you that she does something nice for me every single time we eat out or shop together, for that matter. I've never had any desire to knock my mother flat while lunging for a bill.

However, I've witnessed many close calls between Mom and her cousins and sister-in-law (all of the "girls" on the other side of seventy), so I've decided that this bill-grabbing is a generational thing.

They may look as frail as wrens, but these women transform into tough old buzzards when it comes time to pay.

"My treat today!" Mom chirped to the waitress at a recent outing. "When it's time, just give me the bill, please."

"Oh, no, Kathleen, you're not," said Louise. "You drove, and gas is higher than a cat's back. I'll take that bill, young lady."

The waitress fidgeted with her pencil, starting to worry about this high-maintenance bunch. Then Aunt Vera stuck her oar in.

"It's my turn to pay, anyway, girls," she said. "Kathleen, you treated all of us to ice cream after Viola's funeral."

That comment briefly stalled Mom while she calculated their dining history and bill-paying transactions since that point. Viola died three years ago.

"Vera, you've given me all those tomatoes from your garden and that huckleberry jelly just last month. You've returned the favor tenfold."

Our table was beginning to attract more attention than the three-inch-high coconut cream pie.

Then Lela, whose stomach was rumbling, made a wise suggestion: that each of us pay for our own meal. Louise wouldn't be any part of it.

"That's not right. I invited you girls out and, by golly, I'm paying for the whole bunch," she said.

When the waitress rolled her eyes, the rest of them took pity and agreed: Let Louise buy — this time.

Unfortunately, when it came time to pay, Louise couldn't find her billfold. She had changed to her black pocketbook for this outing, and apparently the billfold hadn't made the switch from her other bag. The rest of them smiled as they dived into their purses for cash for their own meals and divvied the cost of Louise's right down to the penny.

Mom snatched the tab for my club sandwich as it fluttered in the waitress's hand. I didn't raise a fuss. This makes Mom happy.

And it makes me even happier.

The Strong-Willed Mother
Kim Wier

It's settled. If I die tomorrow, an inheritance is secured for my family. They needn't worry about their future. I have a Will.

I won't pretend that I understand every nuance of the document, in part because everyone involved apparently gets a new name. My husband and I were the first to be rechristened. I am Testatrix. He is Executor. It sounds as if we are rulers from the planet Zorg.

All three of my children are henceforth to be known by one common name, Beneficiary. This one I may actually adopt at home. I might appear less senile if I could keep their names straight for a change. I sense their confidence in my mental capacity diminishing each time I tell Bailey to get his homework done, only to hear, "I'm Chase, Mom, remember?"

Now I can just say, "Don't argue with me, Beneficiary, I am Testatrix, ruler of intergalactic discipline."

It isn't just people who have been renamed. My mortgaged house has been elevated to a new position. Instead of a two story with an overgrown lawn, it is an Estate. Even my debts have become nobler. They are no longer just bills; they are now Encumbrances. It's a fitting name, since apparently, even if I die, they get passed along to my heirs.

Other aspects of inheritances are not so simple. In the Will and Testament world, every bequeath, no matter how small, requires a translator. It would be impossible to simply say that I would like my favorite teacup to go to my daughter. This type of request would require an official memorandum directing my Executor to properly dispose of any portion of my personal and household effects according to Article 2 and subject to probate. After all, should anyone contest the teacup issue, it must be able to stand up under judicial scrutiny.

Which brings me to my favorite part of the Will. According to Article 9, "If any beneficiary shall contest the validity of the Will, then all benefits provided for such beneficiary are revoked." In other words, "Don't argue with your mother." You've got to love a document that gives you the last word even from the grave.

Attention, Children:
The Bathroom Door Is Closed!
Becky Freeman

Please do not stand here and talk, whine, or ask questions. Wait until I get out.

Yes, it is locked. I want it that way. It is not broken, I am not trapped.

I know I have left it unlocked, and even open at times, since you were born, because I was afraid some horrible tragedy might occur while I was in there, but it's been years and I want some PRIVACY.

Do not ask me how long I will be. I will come out when I am done.

Do not bring the phone to the bathroom door.

Do not go running back to the phone yelling, "She's in the BATHROOM!"

Do not begin to fight as soon as I go in.

Do not stick your little fingers under the door and wiggle them. This was only funny when you were two.

Do not slide pennies, Legos, or notes under the door. Even when you were two, this got a little tiresome.

If you have followed me down the hall talking, and are still talking as you face this closed door, please turn around, walk away, and wait for me in another room. I will be glad to listen to you when I am done.

Oh ...

And, yes, I still love you.

— Mom

Injured Innocence
Mark Twain

My mother had a good deal of trouble with me, but I think she enjoyed it. She had none at all with my brother Henry, who was two years younger than I, and I think that the unbroken monotony of his goodness and truthfulness and obedience would have been a burden to her but for the relief and variety which I furnished in the other direction. I was a tonic. I was valuable to her. I never thought of it before, but now I see it. I never knew Henry to do a vicious thing toward me, or toward anyone else — but he frequently did righteous ones that cost me as heavily. It was his duty to report me, when I needed reporting and neglected to do it myself, and he was very faithful in discharging that duty....

One day when my mother was not present Henry took sugar from her prized and precious old-English sugar bowl, which was an heirloom in the family — and he managed to break the bowl. It was the first time I had ever had a chance to tell anything on him, and I was inexpressibly glad. I told him I was going to tell on him, but he was not disturbed. When my mother came in and saw the bowl lying on the floor in fragments, she was speechless for a minute. I allowed that silence to work; I judged it would increase the effect. I was waiting for her to ask, "Who did that?" — so that I could fetch out my news. But it was an error of calculation. When she got through with her silence she didn't ask anything about it — she merely gave me a crack on the skull with her thimble that I felt all the way down to my heels. Then I broke out with my injured innocence, expecting to make her very sorry that she had punished the wrong one. I expected her to do something remorseful and pathetic. I told her that I was not the one — it was Henry. But there was no upheaval. She said, without emotion: "It's all right. It isn't any matter. You deserve it for something you've done that I didn't know about; and if you haven't done it, why, then you deserve it for something that you are going to do that I shan't hear about."

A Mother Can't Help Worrying
Mark Twain

I was always told that I was a sickly and precarious and tiresome and uncertain child, and lived mainly on allopathic medicines during the first seven years of my life. I asked my mother about this, in her old age — she was in her eighty-eighth year — and said:

"I suppose that during all that time you were uneasy about me?"

"Yes, the whole time."

"Afraid I wouldn't live?"

After a reflective pause — ostensibly to think out the facts — "No — afraid you would."

10

Adventures in Matrimony

Keep your eyes wide open before marriage, half shut afterwards.

— Benjamin Franklin

I dreamed of a wedding of elaborate elegance, a church filled with family and friends. I asked him what kind of a wedding he wished for; he said one that would make me his wife.

— Anonymous

Any married man should forget his mistakes; there's no use in two people remembering the same thing.

— Anonymous

Nuptial Humor
Various Authors

When our daughter Bethany was four, she attended her first funeral. With her daddy acting as presiding minister, Bethany sat wide-eyed with me, taking in all the people and flowers.

"What's that, Mommy?" she asked as the funeral directors pushed the wheeled casket up to the front.

"That is the man who died," I said. "He went to heaven to be with Jesus."

Bethany nodded. She understood.

Only four days later, Bethany and I attended her first wedding. Once again the people gathered, flowers were everywhere, and Daddy was the pastor. Bethany loved seeing the beautiful bride come down the aisle. "Isn't this a lovely wedding?" I whispered to my young companion.

"But, Mommy," Bethany said, "where is the dead man?"

— Judy Carlsen

The pink wedding bouquet flew toward us. Dressed in our wedding finest, all of us single girls readied ourselves for the mad scramble to catch the bouquet. In the front row were four bridesmaids (including myself) and my eight-year-old sister, Erin. We all jostled for position.

As the bouquet sailed overhead, we leapt for it, arms reaching to the sky. As we landed, our eyes darted back and forth for the lucky girl who had caught it. Looking down, we discovered that it was my little sister!

Erin turned to the bridesmaid next to her, pulled out a pink rose from the bouquet, and said, "Here, Di, maybe now you can get a date."

— Jana Carey

My husband, a pastor, is often asked to officiate at weddings. During one well-booked wedding season, we were preparing for one son's birthday party. When I asked him whom he wanted to invite, the only names he gave were his "girl friends."

"Who are you going to marry when you grow up?" I asked jokingly.

Without hesitation he replied, "When I grow up I'm going to be a pastor and marry them all."

— Marian Obeda

My five-year-old grandnephew was obviously worried as he looked down the long aisle of the church where his aunt was to be married the following day. His grandmother had an idea. "I think I'll give a prize to the person who does the best job tomorrow," she told him.

We were all holding our breath the next day, but when it was time, the ring bearer performed without a hitch.

When his grandmother told him he had won the prize, he was both excited and relieved. "I was pretty sure I had it," he admitted, "until Aunt Dana came in wearing that white dress and the horn was blowing. Then I started thinking — she might win!"

— Barbara Lee

On our first anniversary, after a romantic candlelit dinner, my wife, Elizabeth, emerged from the kitchen with the finishing touch: the top of our wedding cake for dessert. At the first cut, the iced layer "squeaked" at us. For an entire year, we had saved a round chunk of frosting-covered Styrofoam in our freezer!

— Don Singleton

At the spring wedding of an older couple, my parents waited with the rest of the guests for the celebration to begin. The church organist played through her entire repertoire of wedding songs, but nothing happened. Not wanting to repeat herself, she continued with Easter hymns in keeping with the season. Soon the door to the pastor's study opened. A shaky, ashen groom appeared just as the organist completed the first line of "Up from the Grave He Arose."

— Sharon Espeseth

While attending a marriage seminar dealing with communication, Tom and his wife, Grace, listened to the instructor. "It is essential that husbands and wives know the things that are important to each other." He addressed the men. "Can you describe your wife's favorite flower?"

Tom leaned over, touched his wife's arm gently, and whispered, "It's Pillsbury, isn't it?"

— Anonymous

A couple drove down a country road for several miles, not saying a word.

An earlier discussion had led to an argument, and neither of them wanted to concede their position. As they passed a barnyard full of mules, goats, and pigs, the husband asked sarcastically, "Relatives of yours?"

"Yep," the wife replied, "in-laws."

— Anonymous

A husband read an article to his wife about how many words women use a day — thirty thousand to a man's fifteen thousand.

The wife replied, "The reason has to be because we have to repeat everything to men."

The husband then turned to his wife and asked, "What?"

— Anonymous

A man and his wife were having an argument about who should brew the coffee each morning.

The wife said, "You should do it, because you get up first, and then we don't have to wait as long to get our coffee."

The husband said, "You are in charge of cooking around here and you should do it, because that is your job, and I can just wait for my coffee."

Wife replies, "No, you should do it, and besides, it is in the Bible that the man should do the coffee."

Husband replies, "I can't believe that; show me."

So she fetched the Bible, opened the New Testament, and showed him at the top of several pages that it indeed says ... "HEBREWS."

— Anonymous

Old aunts used to come up to me at weddings, poking me in the ribs and cackling, telling me, "You're next." They stopped when I started doing the same thing to them at funerals.

— Anonymous

Mom's Last Laugh
Robin Lee Shope

Consumed by my loss, I didn't notice the hardness of the pew where I sat. I was at the funeral of my dearest friend — my mother. She finally had lost her long battle with cancer. The hurt was so intense, I found it hard to breathe at times.

Always supportive, Mother clapped loudest at my school plays, held a box of tissues while listening to my first heartbreak, comforted me at my father's death, encouraged me in college, and prayed for me my entire life.

When Mother's illness was diagnosed, my sister had a new baby and my brother had recently married his childhood sweetheart, so it fell to me, the twenty-seven-year-old middle child without entanglements, to take care of her. I counted it an honor.

"What now, Lord?" I asked, sitting in church. My life stretched out before me as an empty abyss.

My brother sat stoically with his face toward the cross while clutching his wife's hand. My sister sat slumped against her husband's shoulder, his arms around her as she cradled their child. All so deeply grieving, no one noticed I sat alone.

My place had been with our mother, preparing her meals, helping her walk, taking her to the doctor, seeing to her medication, reading the Bible together. Now she was with the Lord.

My work was finished, and I was alone.

Suddenly I heard a door open and slam shut at the back of the church. Quick footsteps hurried along the carpeted floor. An exasperated young man looked around briefly and then sat next to me. He folded his hands and placed them on his lap. His eyes were brimming with tears. He began to sniffle.

"I'm late," he explained, though no explanation was necessary.

After several eulogies, he leaned over and commented, "Why do they keep calling Mary by the name of 'Margaret'?"

"Because that was her name, Margaret. Never Mary. No one called her 'Mary,'" I whispered. I wondered why this person couldn't have sat on the other side of the church. He interrupted my grieving with his tears and fidgeting. Who was this stranger anyway?

"No, that isn't correct," he insisted, as several people glanced over at us whispering. "Her name is Mary, Mary Peters."

"That isn't who this is."

"Isn't this the Lutheran church?"

"No, the Lutheran church is across the street."

"Oh."

"I believe you're at the wrong funeral, sir."

The solemnity of the occasion mixed with the realization of the man's mistake bubbled up inside me and came out as laughter. I cupped my hands over my face, hoping it would be interpreted as sobs.

The creaking pew gave me away. Sharp looks from other mourners only made the situation seem more hilarious. I peeked at the bewildered, misguided man seated beside me. He was laughing too as he glanced around, deciding it was too late for an uneventful exit. I imagined Mother laughing.

At the final "Amen," we darted out a door and into a parking lot.

"I do believe we'll be the talk of the town," he said smiling. He said his name was Rick and, since he had missed his aunt's funeral, asked me out for a cup of coffee.

That afternoon began a lifelong journey for me with this man who attended the wrong funeral but was in the right place. A year after our meeting, we were married at a country church where he was the assistant pastor. This time we both arrived at the same church, right on time.

In my time of sorrow, God gave me laughter. In place of loneliness, God gave me love. This past June we celebrated our twenty-second wedding anniversary.

Whenever anyone asks us how we met, Rick tells them, "Her mother and my aunt Mary introduced us, and it's truly a match made in heaven."

Get on Your Trike and Ride
Ken Davis

Being the father of two girls isn't an easy role in our society. The toughest part comes when boys begin taking an interest in your daughters. Handling that crisis demands wisdom and discernment.

I remember the first boy who walked brazenly up to my door and asked if Traci could come over to his house. I told him my daughter wasn't that kind of girl. "You have a lot of nerve," I said. "I don't want to see you hanging around here anymore." He took it quite well, got on his red tricycle, and rode away.

Because I remembered my own teen years when my adolescent hormones outnumbered the brain cells in my body, I projected my distrust on any male child who could walk. If the male in question had a car, the distrust increased tenfold. If he owned a van, I sought to keep him outside the city limits.

Several years after the tricycle incident, I was helping Diane clear the table when another young man darkened my threshold. I watched through the window as he approached the house and chickened out twice. It could have been my reputation had gotten around. Whatever the case, he was trying to work up the courage to ring the bell. As he approached the third time, I tiptoed to the door and slowly turned the knob. When I heard the boy step up to the doorbell, I yanked the door open and thundered, "WHAT DO YOU WANT?"

The boy leaped back, his eyes as big and shiny as compact discs. I realized I was still holding a large butcher knife in each hand. I'll give him credit for this much — he approached again. "Can Traci come out, or can I come in?" he stammered.

"Do you now own, or did you ever own, a red tricycle?" I growled, rubbing the edges of the two knives together. Before he could answer, I tapped one of the knives on the screen door. "You look a lot like the kid that killed my parents." He backed away several steps. "I'm just kidding," I said with a high-pitched cackle. "I killed my own parents — come on in!"

He did. But I'm sure the word spread about the Davis girls' dad. Many of the boys who came over later would stand some distance from the door and shout with crackling voices, "Is anybody home?" Some never got out of their car. ...

Recently my youngest daughter, beautifully dressed in white, stood beside me at the back of the church. Standing at the front of the church was the young man who was about to become her husband. I couldn't have done a better job if I'd picked him myself. Yet despite his strong character and wonderful reputation, I was still the father. As much as I'd grown to love him, I still looked at him as the pervert who stole my little baby girl. But I wasn't the one in control here. I was never really the one in control. As we stood waiting for the ceremony to begin, she squeezed my arm and whispered, "I love you."

I found out later that she didn't say it because she loved me (even though she surely does). She and her sister had made a bet that they could make me cry during the ceremony.

I didn't cry. It did throw me off though. When the pastor asked, "Who giveth this woman to this man?" I answered, "My mother and I do."

After a wonderful reception, they left on their honeymoon. The four-wheel-drive vehicle they took to the mountains was packed with gifts, camping equipment, and clothing. As they drove away, I thought I saw — packed in the very back, beneath a backpack — a red tricycle.

11

Laughter: The Secret to a Good Marriage

My husband gave me a mood ring the other day.
When I'm in a good mood, it turns green. When I'm in
a bad mood, it leaves a red mark on his forehead.

— Anonymous

A wedding anniversary is the celebration of love, trust, partnership,
tolerance, and tenacity. The order varies for any given year.

— Paul Sweeney

Oops!
William Ritner

*C*hris, one of my wife's coworkers, was late for work. As she approached an intersection where she needed to turn, she crossed over the white line before the turn lane began. While waiting in traffic, her foot slipped off the brake, and she bumped the car in front of her ... a police car!

The officer got out and scolded her for crossing the white line.

"I knew I had to get over into the turn lane," Chris explained. "Besides, everyone else was doing it."

"Just because every other dimwit does it, doesn't mean you have to do it," the officer replied.

Right then, another car did the exact same thing. The officer left Chris to speak with the newest offender. Moments later, he returned, shaking his head. "That was my wife!" Of course, neither she nor Chris was ticketed.

She's Got Her Bases Covered
Dan Clark

◎

I have an older aunt who has been married four times — first to a banker, then an entertainer, a preacher, and a funeral director. When asked why she had married that many times and to such a diverse mix of men, she had a great reply. "One for the money, two for the show, three to get ready, and four to go!"

Five Golden Decades … Give or Take a Day or Two
Ursula Turner

As lifestyle editor of our local paper, I prepare engagement, wedding, and anniversary announcements. One anniversary announcement I received confused me. It said that Mr. and Mrs. John Smith (not their real names) would be celebrating their fiftieth wedding anniversary. It went on to say that John Smith and Jane Jones were married in 1950 in Coffeyville, Kansas, John on June 3, and Jane on June 5.

I immediately phoned. When the couple's son answered, I asked him about the discrepancy in dates, assuming it was an error.

"The dates are correct," he said. "You may publish them that way."

Baffled, I asked him why his parents didn't check the date on their marriage license if they weren't certain.

"They can't do that," he replied. "Because then one of them would have to admit to having been wrong all these years."

Time to Listen
Phil Callaway

An elderly couple enjoyed a rather opulent sixtieth wedding anniversary put on by their four children and many grandchildren. After the celebration, the husband saw his faithful companion of sixty years across the room. Though he loved her dearly, he remembered again how he had been concerned about her hearing problems lately. Since she was facing the other way, he thought he'd test her.

"Honey," he said from the other side of the room.

She didn't say anything, so he shuffled a few steps closer.

"Honey," he said again.

Still no response.

"Honey," he said a third time, "can you hear me?"

Again there was no reply. So he moved right behind her and whispered, "Honey."

At last she turned to him and said, "For the fourth time, what do you want?"

A Sweet Way to Celebrate
Angel McKay

On Valentine's Day, my husband and I were busy signing cards and preparing sweets when our pastor called. Our eight-year-old son James answered and innocently said, "Mom and Dad are in the bedroom doing the Valentine thing."

When my husband Howard returned the call, our pastor had quite a chuckle. Our Valentine's thing was actually getting treats ready for the kids.

The Truth and Nothing But the Truth
Dan Clark

A police officer pulled over an older couple and said, "You were speeding and you weren't wearing your seat belts."

The elderly man scoffed and replied, "Prove it. I just took off the belt to talk to you!"

Nonplussed, the officer turned to the wife. "Ma'am, your husband was speeding, and he didn't have his seat belt on, now, did he?"

"Officer," she replied, "after forty years of marriage I've learned never to argue with my husband when he's been drinking!"

Nice Try
Margaret Gunn

My friend Margaret mentioned that her husband George never could remember their wedding anniversary on March 7. One year, when they were en route to Australia, at five minutes before midnight on March 6, George proudly looked at Margaret and said, "This year I remembered. Just five minutes."

At that moment the captain's voice announced, "We have crossed the International Date Line. It's now March 8."

Didn't I Tell You?
Dave Meurer

◎

Dale grabbed the ringing phone, listened for a moment, and replied, "You're delivering *what*? Are you sure? Just a moment, please."

She then looked at me with absolute bewilderment, her brow deeply etched.

"Why am I being asked if we are ready to have a refrigerator delivered?" she whispered with her hand cupped over the mouth-piece.

"Well, they probably wanted to make sure we were home," I replied. "Tell them it's fine."

"What are you *talking* about? What refrigerator?"

"The new one, obviously," I replied. "They certainly wouldn't be delivering the old one."

I had to take over the phone lest Dale sound completely irrational.

"They'll be here in thirty minutes," I said after I'd hung up. "Boy, did you sound grumpy on the phone. Did someone wake up on the wrong side of the bed?"

Dale took a very deep breath.

"Dave, I am going to try to be very calm. Let's take it from the top. This is the first I have heard about a new refrigerator."

"Dale, we talked about this last week!" I protested.

"I have NO IDEA what you are talking about!" she exclaimed, throwing her hands in the air.

This was yet another disturbing example of Dale's poor listening skills.

"Dale, don't you remember when I asked if you thought the rose-bushes next to the side gate were too bushy to get something big by them?"

"Y-e-s," she replied cautiously. "I was going to ask why you wanted to know, when you ran out the door to go to work and we never finished the conversation."

"Ohhhh. That's right. I *was* running late. I remember now. But, still, refrigerators are *big*. So you really should have put two and two together."

She made a sound remarkably akin to a deep-sea pearl diver coming up for air before she replied.

"So I was supposed to translate a question about *overgrown rosebushes* into a statement that we are having a *refrigerator* delivered this morning? Not only is that *sheer lunacy*, but did you happen to notice that I just got out of the shower, my hair is all wet, our current refrigerator is full of food, and we are supposed to drive eighty miles to meet Scott and Becky — whom we have not seen for an entire year — in just a few hours?"

I grimaced.

"Hon, it sounds like you bit off more than you can chew," I said. "If today was a bad day for a delivery, it would have been helpful if you would have said something earlier. I think you need to work on your communication skills. I mean, I'm not a mind reader."

She took a series of deep breaths. Personally, I thought this was an odd time to begin practicing her pregnancy breathing techniques, as she had not been expecting for fifteen years. But I decided that could wait for another conversation, as she was starting to give me "the look."

Unfortunately, the refrigerator episode is not the first time Dale's communication weaknesses have been on parade. There was also the incident wherein I added flour to the shopping list and she failed to ask any of the logical follow-up questions that would have revealed that I signed her up to make cupcakes for Brad's second-grade class. Fortunately, Brad reminded her the next morning on the way to school. Although she managed to complete the task on time, the fact remains that she could have avoided zipping around the kitchen like a hyperactive poodle if she had simply asked me about it earlier.

Compounding the problem, Dale is very resistant to accepting responsibility for her consistent communication lapses. I keep telling her that this little flaw is nothing to be ashamed of, and that it merely requires more personal discipline to overcome. But this is one of her little "blind spots," ranking right up there with her tendency to forget to ask me if there are any checks I have not yet recorded before she tries to use the ATM card at the store. You'd think she would learn after a while.

It's a good thing that at least one of us is a good communicator, or our life would be in complete disarray.

Because I am an extremely effective communicator, I have the added advantage of being able to economize on words but still fully cover the topic under discussion. Dale has yet to master this technique, as seen in the following example.

DALE: "Honey, sometimes I feel like, well, I'm drifting in life. I wonder what my role is. I mean, sure, I love you and I love our family, and I believe that God wants me to primarily focus my energy on you and the kids, but I wonder if I am unconsciously avoiding something big. It isn't that I am *unhappy*; it's more like *unsure*. I mean, this is my one shot at life. Am I missing some kind of calling, some kind of bigger picture? Am I actually fulfilling the niche that God has in mind for me, or am I only doing a small part of it? But then on the other hand, I start to wonder if I am just feeling insecure because you are always doing these big projects and meeting with all these important people, while most of my life is spent in a support role. Not that a support role isn't important. And I really do get a lot of satisfaction out of helping you and the kids succeed and grow. But can you see what I mean? Does my life really have value in the big scheme of things? Am I making any real, lasting difference in any significant way? Can you understand how I feel?"

ME: "Sure!"

Lesser communicators would feel compelled to carry on at great length, groping for words and restating in a hundred different ways that, yes, they really understand. They could use up an *entire evening* dealing with this subject. But notice how in that single, efficient monosyllable of "Sure!" I managed to compact a truckload of empathy and compassion and understanding into a single manageable communication unit no larger than a standard vitamin.

Regrettably, most women (Dale included) have not mastered this powerful communication skill, nor do they show any likelihood whatsoever of doing so. This appears to be a genetic flaw in their gender.

While guys know exactly what they mean when they say "Sure!" wives literally have no clue. So, in deference to their weakness in this area, it falls to the guy to stoop down to her inefficient, time-consuming, lower communication ability and fully translate "Sure!" so that women can grasp it.

In the aforementioned case, the translation went like this:

ME: "Dale, I think you have it a *lot* harder than I do. And I think I understand why you are feeling a little unsettled and inse-cure. I have a more well-defined role out in the world, and my job puts me in the limelight sometimes. But, honey, I couldn't make it without you. I would be so lost. You are the calm at the center of the storm, and I rely on you more than you can possibly know. It isn't just all the support stuff you do, taking care of our home and doing all the basic stuff that makes it possible for us to have a comfortable life; it is *who you are* for me. I believe with all my heart and soul that you are a blessing from God. And what you do for the kids and me is really, really, really important, even though you may not always be able to see it, and even if we forget sometimes to tell you. Everyone sees the astronauts on TV, but we forget that there are hundreds and hundreds of people working behind the scenes or they would *never* get off the ground. So you are Houston Control, and I know it, even if the world doesn't. Thanks for being there. I love you."

It may not be efficient, but at least they understand it. And, unlike large appliance deliveries, they'll gladly take it even if it is unexpected.

12

It Seemed Like a Good Idea at the Time...

Some of us learn from other people's mistakes;
the rest of us have to be the other people.

— Barbara Johnson

Why do you necessarily have to be wrong just because
a few million people think you are?

— Frank Zappa

But Doesn't Everyone Call Them "Father"?
George Burns

One summer, when I was seven years old, before I started singing with the Peewee Quartet, I hit upon the idea of going into the ice business. When it's hot, everybody needs ice.

I made myself a pull cart out of an apple crate and two old baby-buggy wheels. I nailed a stick onto the front to pull it, and I'd haul my cart down to an icehouse by the East River and buy a hundred-pound cake of ice for five cents. Then I'd pull it back to my neighborhood, split the cake into four quarters, and sell each one for five cents. I was making a fifteen-cent profit on every cake of ice. By hustling, I would be able to do this three times a day, which meant I could make a profit of $2.25 in a five-day week.

Unfortunately, I never made it to the end of the first week. In order to get to the icehouse I had to go right through the middle of this Italian neighborhood, and on the fourth day I was happily running along with my second cake of ice when these two rough-looking kids stopped me. Right away I knew I was in trouble when one of them said, "Hey, kid, I never saw you in this neighborhood! What's your name?"

I knew I had to come up with an Italian name, so I blurted out the only one I could think of: "Enrico Caruso!"

The bigger of the two stuck his face right in front of mine and snarled, "Are you Catholic?"

I looked right back at him and said, "Are you kidding? My father's a priest!"

That was the end of my ice business. They took my cart and my ice and chased me all the way back to Rivington Street.

The Attic Fiasco
Nancy Kennedy

ⓢ

Technically, it was my husband's fault. He had sworn *never* to allow me into his sacred domain, the attic, ever again. That's fine with me. I don't even like going anywhere near the dusty, cobwebby depository for all the macho man-toys that I've suggested he not keep in the house. (No, dear. I *don't* think a stuffed toad "goes" with the dried flower arrangement on the coffee table. But I do think it would "go" great in the attic — right next to your lucky Bavarian stein.) You know how it is.

Like I said, I normally stay away from the attic, but since no one else was around to help Barry with his annual lugging down of the Christmas tree and boxes of holiday decorations, I became designated helper by default.

"Are you sure you want to do this?" I asked him. "I mean, after what happened last time?"

Last time occurred way back when, in the early years of our marriage when we were eager to be each other's partner and helper. Now, after twenty-four years, we still want that ... just not in the attic. That last time, we had gone up in the attic to run an electrical cable from one end of the house to the other. Barry's job was to crawl through the dust and spiders; mine was to hold the flashlight. That's always my job — to hold the flashlight. Or the ladder. Or the drill box. That day I had an added responsibility — to stay on the rafters.

Now, I'm an intelligent woman. I know that the Beatles' first American hit was "I Want to Hold Your Hand" and that Benjamin Harrison was our first president with a fear of electricity. I can even use the word *zoophyte* in everyday conversation (as in, "Haha, Barry! With a triple word score, *zoophyte* gives me seventy-five points and I win!").

Clearly, I have an extensive vocabulary. But to be honest, I'm not sure what "rafters" are. (Well, I am now, but I wasn't then.)

We climbed up into the attic. Barry handed me the flashlight and showed me where to stand, then crawled off with a spool of wire in his hand. Every so often he'd call out, "Shine it to the left" or "Raise it up an inch."

As a newlywed, it was not the bonding moment I'd hoped it would be. So I sulked. *Any idiot can do this.* Then I looked around for something to occupy myself with since Barry was all the way across the attic and not paying attention to me. That's when I noticed something like sawdust on the attic floor.

I stepped one foot off the board I was standing on and rubbed the "sawdust" with my shoe. "Tea for two, and two for tea," I sang and did a one-footed version of a soft-shoe dance.

I tried the other foot. "Me for you, and you for me."

Next, I tried it with both feet. "Da-da-dah, ta-tah, do-doooo."

As I went to my grand finale, I discovered exactly what rafters are and why one should stay on them when told to do so. It seemed my dance floor was made of Sheetrock, and unlike rafters — sturdy, hurricane-force-wind-resistant wooden beams — Sheetrock isn't designed to hold a 140-pound dancing fool. (I discovered that fact somewhere around the time my right foot went crashing through to the laundry room below.) As I hung there, one leg dangling, I considered not alerting Barry to the situation (in case he should not find it amusing). But, ever observant, he spied me anyway and made his way through the maze of wood and dust.

"Are you okay?" he asked as he reached my side.

When I assured him I was (aside from being up to my thigh in trouble), he breathed a sigh of relief . . . then exploded.

"Didn't I tell you to stay on the rafters?"

"Well, yeah, but . . ."

"Do you think I tell you these things just to hear myself talk?"

Actually, I had considered that once or twice, but this didn't seem to be the best time or place to bring it up. I shrugged my shoulders, brushed Sheetrock dust off my leg, and rubbed my scraped knee.

Barry set me up on the rafter, peeked through our new laundry room skylight, and shrugged. Then he grunted. Loudly.

I took that to mean he didn't want to see my soft-shoe. I gulped. "Are we done up here?"

He continued to grunt and make unintelligible noises. These I interpreted to mean, yes, as far as Barry was concerned, I was finished. For the day, anyway. At least we got another project out of the shoe fiasco — patching the hole and retexturing and repainting the laundry room ceiling — which I didn't mind a bit. The truth is, when I'm not crashing through ceilings, Barry and I work well together. Which is a good thing, considering what happened the day we returned to the attic.

Once again, all I had to do was hold the flashlight and *stay on the rafters*. But, well ... I sort of ... didn't, and ... um ... well, I've always wanted a skylight in the kitchen.

Pinching People to Jesus
Marsha Marks

I used to think you could *make* people come to Jesus. My approach to evangelism was to tell people they needed to come to Jesus and if they said no, I pinched them. This "come to Jesus or I'll kill you" method was most evident in my first target: my brother Joe.

When I was nine and Joe was eight, I was big for my age and he was little for his. Thus, he did whatever I told him. But usually he put up some kind of verbal fight. (Years later, in college, he would become a national debate champion — a skill he honed with me.)

When I first heard the good news of God sending his Son to die for our sins, I wanted everyone to "get saved." And my plan was to start with Joe. So I made him come to church with me and I allowed him to sit through one entire sermon without pressuring him to respond. He didn't respond, so that evening in our little church in northwest Washington State, I told him either he went forward to become a Christian or he'd be sorry. And I pinched him, for good measure.

He looked right at me and said, "No."

"Yes," I said.

"No," he said. (His debating skills weren't perfected yet.)

"Yes," I said, and pinched him again. "Go!" I said. The congregation was singing the second verse, and we didn't have a lot of time. *"Go!"* I said again.

"No!" he said. This went on for one full minute. Finally, twenty-three pinches later, each one more painful than the last, my brother went forward. I went with him, pinching him all the way down the aisle.

The minister looked at my brother and saw what he assumed to be the fear of God in his eyes. "Do you want to receive Jesus?" he said.

"Yes, he does," I said.

And right there the minister had my brother repeat a simple prayer, which I took to be a success. I had succeeded where the Holy Spirit had failed. I'd forced my brother into the kingdom of God.

Years later my brother told me he hadn't really received Jesus that day.

"But you went forward!" I said, wondering if I should start pinching him again.

"Change doesn't come by going through the motions. It has to come from inside," he said. "It's a personal choice. God gave us free will."

As I've grown up in my faith, one of the most shocking things I've learned about evangelism is that Jesus never pinched anyone into the kingdom. If someone came to him, they did it freely, and if they didn't come, he left them in their choices — choices with eternal consequences, but still he honored people by allowing them to say no.

I want to be more like that. I want to love people so much that when they say no, I respect their answer as their choice. I can still go off alone and pray for them in secret. But I don't want to pinch anybody to Jesus because I want to be like him, and the Bible says, "God's kindness leads you toward repentance" (Romans 2:4).

The Holy Terrors
Rachael Phillips

◎

It began with nothing to do on a Sunday night after church.

When I heard our front door's creak and Aunt Iddy's voice, I turned on *The Lawrence Welk Show*, knowing full well my cousins' church frowned on watching television. Bobby and Cissy were just beginning their dance routine, dipping and swirling in a way that would surely be considered an official abomination before the Lord. I felt a rush of satisfaction.

My oldest cousin, fifteen-year-old Starreen, dutifully avoided the cramped screen, with only an occasional glance. Lurleen, her sister, only bothered to sin when a good-looking man peddled Aqua Velva After Shave. Darleen stared unabashedly until Aunt Iddy hollered for her to "stop lookin' at that tee-vee!"

I loved my cousins, but I relished their occasional falls into pits of dissipation. They often warned me that my short hair and white Levi's would surely send me to perdition. So I made it my business to see they achieved no heavenly brownie points while in my presence.

Tonight, however, I was not satisfied to watch my cousins merely lose the pinnacle of Paradise. I wanted to take them down.

"Let's sneak into the drive-in," I whispered.

The huge screen rose seven blocks away, mighty as Nebuchadnezzar's golden idol. I had once viewed Walt Disney's *Lady and the Tramp* at the drive-in, but mostly, my family passed it on the way to church or school. We children gaped, fascinated, as jungle elephants or warplanes rampaged across the screen. Sometimes a monolithic Doris Day captured us with her song for three seconds before black cornfields swallowed her whole. As I grew older, I regarded the avoidance of the drive-in as a silent Eleventh Commandment. To my cousins, it personified evil at its slimiest.

It was perfect.

Starreen's glass-green eyes stared, dark with worry. But she always looked worried. It was part of her job description as the oldest.

"What's on?" Lurleen whispered.

"James Bond," I replied.

"Ya'll shouldn't do this," ten-year-old Darleen whimpered, scratching her mosquito bites. Bugs always bit her on the face.

"Then stay here," I told her. "But don't breathe a word, or we'll tell Ronnie Lee you love him."

Darleen had pledged undying devotion to Ronnie Lee Simmons by writing his name in the playground dust fifty times. Her freckled face faded to white. "I won't tell."

"We're goin' for a walk outside where it's cool, Aunt Iddy," I sang out.

"Ya-ll really *can* do somethin' besides watch that *tee-vee*."

I pushed Starreen out the door before she could kneel and confess.

Her hair-spray-stiff dome of dark hair quivered, but she showed no signs of recanting.

"How do we get through the bushes?" Lurleen asked.

I rolled my eyes. "Get down on your knees and crawl!"

"I'm wearing a dress!"

My cousins always wore dresses. While I cherished the thought of adding to their transgressions by ruining their church clothes, their lack of mobility might hamper us. For the first time, I felt pangs of doubt.

"You can do it." I slithered between thorny limbs into a parallel universe. Blood spurted from tiny punctures in my arms, but the scene before me anesthetized my pain. The cement-block concession stand in all its neon glory beckoned — heaven! Whiffs of butter-soaked popcorn and steaming chili dogs made me quiver.

"I can't get through!" Starreen wailed.

"Push between the branches," Lurleen said impatiently. Like me, she stood bewitched by the carnival of smells, sights, and sounds. An eight-foot-high tuxedoed James Bond gave us a gleaming smile from the screen. "*Lookit* him." She all but drooled. My knees melted.

"Lurleena Priscilla Fuller, I don't want to hear no more," Starreen said. "My hair's caught. Help me out of here. We're going *back*."

"Starreen, are you gonna tell Mom?" The sky, a ceiling full of God's eyes, glimmered coldly at me.

"Only if you don't help me."

Lurleen sighed; we hunkered down and began slowly loosening Starreen's hair from the thorns.

Suddenly a gun's thunderclap exploded above our heads.

"GET OUT OF HERE, YOU KIDS!" said a godlike voice. Lurleen and I had already bulleted halfway home, with Starreen, wearing branches like antlers in her beehive, not far behind. She set a new world record for the two-hundred-yard dash in patent leather high heels. We picked each other's leaves and stanched each other's blood, then entered my house so quietly our parents hardly heard us. I turned the television off. Darleen opened her mouth to squawk, but one unison look from us silenced her. We sat.

"Want some Kool-Aid?" Mom asked.

We shook our heads. And sat.

If this were a Sunday school story from my childhood, we would have learned our lesson, never to sin again. It's not, and we didn't.

But years later, I still can't bring myself to watch James Bond movies — unless, that is, I'm headed to church and just happen to take the route that goes straight past the drive-in.

Someone Needs a Time-Out
John Ortberg

Some years ago we traded in my old Volkswagen Super Beetle for our first piece of new furniture: a mauve sofa. It was roughly the shade of Pepto-Bismol, but because it represented to us a substantial investment, we thought "mauve" sounded better.

The man at the furniture store warned us not to get it when he found out we had small children. "You don't want a mauve sofa," he advised. "Get something the color of dirt." But we had the naïve optimism of young parenthood. "We know how to handle our children," we said. "Give us the mauve sofa."

From that moment on, we all knew clearly the number one rule in the house. Don't sit on the mauve sofa. Don't touch the mauve sofa. Don't play around the mauve sofa. Don't eat on, breathe on, look at, or think about the mauve sofa. Remember the forbidden tree in the Garden of Eden? "On every other chair in the house you may freely sit, but upon this sofa, the mauve sofa, you may not sit, for in the day you sit thereupon, you shall surely die."

Then came the Fall.

One day there appeared on the mauve sofa a stain. A red stain. A red jelly stain.

So my wife, who had chosen the mauve sofa and adored it, lined up our three children in front of it: Laura, age four, and Mallory, two and a half, and Johnny, six months.

"Do you see that, children?" she asked. "That's a stain. A red stain. A red jelly stain. The man at the sofa store says it is not coming out. Not forever. Do you know how long forever is, children? That's how long we're going to stand here until one of you tells me who put the stain on the mauve sofa."

Mallory was the first to break. With trembling lips and tear-filled eyes she said, "Laura did it." Laura passionately denied it. Then there was silence, for the longest time. No one said a word. I knew the children wouldn't, for they had never seen their mother so upset. I knew they wouldn't, because they knew that if they did, they would spend eternity in the time-out chair.

I knew they wouldn't, because *I* was the one who put the red jelly stain on the mauve sofa, and I knew I wasn't saying anything. I figured I would find a safe place to confess — such as in a book I was going to write, maybe.

Good Knight!

George Burns

During one of my many trips to London, I became friends with a very wealthy, yet very modest, Jewish chap named Hyman Goldfarb. On one visit, Hy told me that because of his large donations to charities through the years, the queen wanted to knight him, but he was going to turn it down.

"That's a great honor," I said. "Why would you turn it down?"

"Because during the ceremony you have to say something in Latin," he said. "And I don't wish to bother studying Latin just for that."

"So say something in Hebrew. The queen wouldn't know the difference."

"Brilliant," Hy complimented me, "but what should I say?"

"Remember that question the son asks the father on the first night of Passover?...'Why is this night different from all other nights?' Can you say that in Hebrew?"

"Of course," he said. "*Ma nishtana ha leila hazeh.* Thank you, old sport. I shall become a knight."

At the ceremony Hy waited his turn while several of the other honorees went before the queen. Finally they called his name. He knelt before Her Majesty, and she placed her sword on one shoulder and then on the other and motioned for Hy to speak.

Out came "*Ma nishtana ha leila hazeh.*"

The queen turned to her husband and said, "Why is this knight different from all other knights?"

13

Did I Just Do That?

Better to trip with the feet than with the tongue.

— Zeno of Citium

The greatest mistake you can make in life is to be continually fearing you will make one.

— Elbert Hubbard

Lost and Found
Marsha Marks

I am forever losing the keys to my car. (And may I make a social observation here? Have you noticed that in any given family, there is one person who loses the keys and one person who doesn't? What is the deal with that?) But, back to my specific problem. I have five sets of keys to my one car and I can never find one set. My husband has one set of keys to his one car, and he has never lost his keys. (I've never even seen him looking for them unless I have used them because I couldn't find mine and then lost them before I could return them to him.)

The deal is, and this is oh-so-embarrassing to admit, one time I lost one set, went into the house to get a spare, and was driving through town when someone flagged me down. When I opened my window to ask the person what she wanted, she pointed to the passenger door and said, "KEYS. YOUR KEYS ARE HANGING IN THE DOOR LOCK." And so it was that I had left my keys in the passenger side door, forgotten they were there, and gone into the house to look for them, and when I couldn't find them, I got another set and drove off, hearing a banging on the side of the door and thinking we really needed to get this car in for repair.

If God saves everything we have lost, I have no doubt there will be a mountain of keys awaiting me in heaven.

The Roar of Laughter
Susan Duke

Have you ever had one of those embarrassing moments in the presence of friends that ends up marking you for life? My friend Kathy and her husband, Emery, will never let me live down one of those "sacred" moments that occurred when my husband, Harvey, and I were visiting their church.

They have now renamed me Tiger Woman.

It's bad enough that we were seated in the enormous sanctuary's second row, but worse that we were surrounded on all sides by members. When the enthusiastically charged pastor asked the congregation to stand and repeat some of the hearty and valid points he'd be making in his sermon, I jumped right in with the responsive crowd.

"I'm here because I love the Lord!" we all repeated after the dynamic leader.

"And I'm a tither, not a robber!" the pastor continued ... and we responded again.

Except this time, for whatever reason, my ears didn't hear exactly what the pastor said. In trying to follow the flow of the moment, my mouth spontaneously repeated what my ears "thought" they heard.

"I'm a *tiger*, not a robber!" I exclaimed.

The look on Kathy's face as she turned to me was enough to make us both double over with hysterical laughter. When she finally came up for air and explained to her baffled husband what we were laughing about, the laughter only escalated ... finally reaching my poor red-faced husband, who was trying to remain proper!

It was one of those rare moments when you thank God for friends with whom you can laugh and be silly and miraculously redeem some sense of dignity.

I smile each time I open my e-mail and find a message from Kathy addressed to Tiger Woman. I'm reminded of the joy of friendship when I look at the small stuffed beanie tiger that sits on my computer monitor and the large orange striped tiger magnet that graces my refrigerator door and growls whenever I press its head. Both are compliments of Kathy and Emery — friends who give me the freedom to *roar* with sacred laughter!

Embarrassment —
Life's Natural Blush
Becky Freeman

Ⓔ

I thought all family reunions proceeded like ours. First comes the food. In the Jones family, sugar was always our main course.

Once we had our fill of sugar and caffeine, aunts, uncles, cousins, grandmas, and grandpas would stumble into the living room for the last course: storytelling. More specifically, we gathered together to tell the most embarrassing thing that had happened to us in the previous year.

My mother always came to these family sessions fully loaded (with stories, that is). One of my all-time favorite true tales occurred one morning as my mother sat on the porch drinking her coffee. Suddenly a middle-aged woman walked into view. The strange woman, as Mother tells it, was wearing a lime-green bikini and sporting fur-lined boots on her feet. She stopped to chat with Mother, and in the course of the rather awkward conversation, the woman let my mom know that she owned her own business.

"Now, I've learned one thing," the woman told Mother proudly. "I don't hire pretty women. Men can't keep their minds on their work with pretty young things around the office. No, sir. I like to hire ugly old women." Now my mother is a beautiful woman — inside and out — but she had been caught on this particular morning without benefit of makeup to face or brush to hair. At this point, the bikini-clad woman stopped midsentence, took a long look at Mother, sized her up carefully, then paid my mom the supreme compliment. "I'd hire you," she said.

I've lost count of how many times I've heard that story as I was growing up, and I'm still chuckling about it thirty years later. Actually, I was a mother with children of my own before it occurred to me that telling embarrassing stories isn't a part of every family's legacy and tradition.

Pity.

If you grow up knowing that an embarrassing moment can be redeemed into a hilarious story by the year's end, the pain of being mortified gives way to the joy of being a ham. If I have been gifted in this life, I believe it is to have survived more red-faced moments than anyone else on the planet — and still live to tell the tale. Over and over and over again. As a matter of fact, I got so proficient at stumbling into embarrassing situations and telling about them later that eventually I had no choice but to turn it into an income-producing venture.

Nearing midlife, I've survived nearly every conceivable form of embarrassment. I've fallen from platforms — faceup and facedown.

I've unknowingly carried a bag of trash, dangling it daintily from my arm, up and down a crowded mall — believing all the while I was carrying my purse.

I've been shopping for clothes and noticed a sudden chill beneath my waist, then realized — with a start — that my wraparound skirt had come unwrapped.

I've called my husband home to help me retrieve my keys from a locked car — only to discover that the driver's side window had been rolled completely down the entire time.

I've put eye shadow on my lips and lipstick on my eyelids. Spray starched my hair, and hair sprayed my blouses.

At one embarrassing — but very memorable — athletic event, I volunteered to carry a five-gallon container of orange Kool-Aid to the concession stand. Only problem was, with every step across the length of the field, I unwittingly pressed the spigot against my abdomen. I started out the morning dressed mostly in white; I ended up the day wearing mostly orange drink.

You may ask, "Is there no end to these stories?"

No, there is no end.

Then there was the day the elementary principal asked me to come in to discuss my son's problems with his organizational skills and how I might help him "just generally get his act together." After the conference with the principal, I assured her I'd help "get my son together." I walked out of the office and caught a glimpse of my reflection in the office window. My embarrassment blossomed into full red-faced bloom when I realized I'd been reassuring the principal — with a forgotten curler bobbing atop the center of my head.

Need I go on?

I need.

Cars have turned out to be quite the popular vehicle for supplying me with embarrassing material. I've driven off with gasoline pump handles. Absconded with those little bank tubes more times than I can count. I've plowed into so many of our neighbor's mailboxes that my husband keeps several spares on hand. Once a band of teenagers went on one of those reckless sprees, plowing down every mailbox in the neighborhood. The next morning as I drove my children to school, they observed, with mouths agape, all the mailboxes lying on the ground or bent awkwardly at the middle. In unison, my own children accusingly chided, "Mother! How could you!"

I once drove backwards for five miles — in full view of my bewildered neighbors — because I couldn't get my car to go forward. (This threw several dogs into a state of confusion. They so wanted to chase my car — but which way to run?)

Yes, I am an "embarrassment survivor" — of the highest order. When people compare the things they've done with my list of embarrassing scenes, they inevitably back down and admit, "Yes, Becky, you are the Queen of the Red-Faced Moment."

To which I humbly respond, "Well, it's a living."

What Did You Say?
Gracie Malone

It was hot outside — hot enough to cook a two-egg omelet on the sidewalk without a skillet. My friend Carolyn was also flat broke. But she did have a shiny new credit card.

Dripping sweat, her hair hanging in strings, sundress sticking to the back of her legs, Carolyn jumped in her car and headed to town to purchase a fan. She parked in front, bolted through the double doors, waving plastic, and approached a nice-looking college student clerk.

"Sir," she began, "does this store carry ovulating fans?"

The young gentleman didn't crack a grin as he pointed to a nearby shelf, then gently said, "Ma'am, I think they are called oscillating fans."

14

More Fun with Y Chromosomes

If high heels were so wonderful, men would still be wearing them.

— Sue Grafton

Behind every successful man is a surprised woman.

— Maryon Pearson

Quiet Humor
Marsha Marks

My husband is a very reserved man and yet one of the funniest men I know. He is a master of one-liners.

Once Tom and I were being interviewed by a reporter for a magazine. The reporter talked to me for most of an hour, while I bubbled over with all kinds of funny stories. And Tom, in his usual stance, was quiet, simply enjoying the show.

Finally the interviewer turned to him and found out that he was an aerospace engineer and that his mother was a nurse and his father a pharmacist and that they had all been born and raised in a conservative Midwest environment. "Well ...," began the interviewer, trying to sum up my relationship to Tom's relatives, "after hearing about your parents, I can bet Marsha must just be like opening a window for them and letting in a breath of fresh air."

Tom looked her in the eye and said, "I'm not sure they like that much breeze."

Husbandisms
Various Authors

The best way to get most husbands to do something is to suggest that perhaps they're too old to do it.

— Ann Bancroft

My wife and I were happy for twenty years. Then we met.

— Rodney Dangerfield

A good wife always forgives her husband when she's wrong.

— Milton Berle

I was married by a judge. I should have asked for a jury.

— George Burns

When women are depressed, they either eat or go shopping. Men invade another country. It's a whole different way of thinking.

— Elaine Boosler

Never go to bed mad. Stay up and fight.

— Phyllis Diller

Women will never be equal to men until they can walk down the street with a bald head and a big gut and still think they are beautiful.

— Anonymous

It Pays to Know Your Scripture
Janice Walsh

M y pastor-husband Scott has a sweet tooth, so I knew the chocolate chip cookies I'd just baked might disappear before I
returned from running errands.

To discourage him, I taped a verse on the wrapped goodies:
"'Everything is permissible for me' — but not everything is beneficial"
(1 Corinthians 6:12).

When I returned I found half the cookies gone and another
verse attached: "The righteous eat to their hearts' content, but the
stomach of the wicked goes hungry" (Proverbs 13:25).

The Object of His Affection
Barbara Johnson

One lady I read about was planning a romantic evening the day her husband returned from a hunting trip. As he was unpacking his bag in the bedroom, she heard him say, "Oh baby, did I miss you!" Turning around to embrace him, she saw he was kissing the remote control!

Oh, Crumb, He's Watching the Food Network Again
Marti Attoun

Oh, crumb, he's been watching the Food Network again. I studied the grocery list posted on the fridge. Under the usual milk, eggs, bread, my husband had added some items: candied orange peel, dried lavender flowers, shad roe sacs ...

Psychologists and other experts have harped for years about the dangers of a steady diet of television. A glut can create unrealistic expectations and blur what's real and what's fiction. They were warning about kids, though.

I'm living with a grown-up statistic.

I thought nothing of it the first time the stat settled down with his bag of Fritos and cold cheese sandwich in front of Emeril Lagasse.

"Man, look at that braised duck thigh," he mumbled to his cheese. "Even that Portuguese kale soup looks delicious."

Recipe by recipe, the celebrity chefs have whipped up heaping platters of discontent right here in my own kitchen. No longer is the victim content to dine on a microwavable potpie, even when I serve it on Chinet. He suddenly hankers for brie and raspberries in puff pastry and aromatic braised oxtail with preserved lemon polenta. I don't care how many bay leaves you toss on an oxtail, I want no part of it.

Since he started feasting on the cooking shows, the foie gras is greener on the other side, and he fancies himself in the role of celebrity chef with decent cutlery and such. He hasn't actually prepared one of the recipes, but he's in the preheating stage — taking notes and gathering ingredients. His grasp of reality is getting as slippery as custard.

The other day, for example, a section of gutter collapsed. It came crashing down and swung outside our family room window. Meanwhile, the victim continued to jot notes on how to pleat a dumpling.

"You know what I'm really craving?" he said one night when he was tuned in to Wolfgang Puck and tuned out of the here and now. "Scallion pancakes with ginger dipping sauce."

"You can't crave something you've never had," I pointed out. "Besides, you'd need a body mint after eating all those scallions."

His second choice was buckwheat blinis.

I stuck a fish stick with tartar dipping sauce under his nose and reminded him that the TV meals were fiction.

"First, no kitchen has that many clean skillets and saucepans. Second, the time is totally out of sync. A team of drudges has spent hours cutting those Chinese jujubes and lime leaves into pretty little ribbons. And who cleans up all that mess, anyway? It'd take us a week to recover from one of those meals."

But it was too late. His eyes glazed like peach-drizzled crumb cake as he added to his grocery list.

If I can find a coupon for shad roe sacs, fine. Otherwise, I'm switching over to The Weather Channel.

One of Those Days
Gracie Malone

It was a typical Monday, until I heard water gurgling in the down-stairs bathroom. Bounding down the stairs to turn off the washer, I shouted, "Septic tank's stopped up again! Call RotoRooter!"

"Oh no," my husband countered, "that costs too much! I'll rent a rooter."

Before I knew it, Joe was back, dressed in a business suit, white shirt, and tie. Beside him a robotic sewer machine stood at attention like a soldier reporting for duty. It had a round belly of coiled cable, an armlike appendage jutting out on one side, and a fearsome hand-shaped claw.

Joe showed me a big red metal button connected to an electri-cal line that powered the robot. My simple task, explained Joe, was to step on the button when he said "Go" and step off when he said "Stop."

"No problem." I nodded in the affirmative and stepped up to do my duty.

"Go," Joe said. I stomped on the switch. Joe patiently guided the robot's arm as it inched its way into the clogged line. As the motor droned rhythmically, my mind shifted gears, thinking of all the other things I had planned to do that day.

"Stop!" Joe shouted.

I did stop, but not soon enough. In horror, I watched the cable backlash around Joe's leg, leaving traces of black muck on his trousers.

"Pay attention!" Joe yelled. Then with a pained look in his eyes, he added, "Gracie, you're not interested in our septic system, are you?"

"I love our septic tank!" I responded in quick defense.

While Joe untangled the cable, I noticed a chill in the air and rubbed at the goose bumps popping up on my arms. "Hon," I said,

"I'm going to leave my post for just a minute and run get a coat." I dashed inside, flung open the folding closet doors, grabbed a jacket, gave the doors a shove, and whirled around. Before I could slip my arm in the sleeve, one door pivoted and fell, whacked my head, then bounced and landed in a crippled heap on the floor. As I walked back outside, warm tears made trails down my dust-covered cheeks. A small goose egg throbbed on my crown. "The sky is falling!" I wailed as I walked toward Joe with open arms. "The closet door just fell on my head!"

Joe held and comforted me, wiping my tears with the back of his cleanest hand. He stifled a laugh, and when I realized it really was pretty funny, we both gave in to a chuckle. Assured that I was consoled and in control of my emotions, Joe turned back to the business at hand. He reinserted the robot's arm into the gaping hole while mumbling, "The joys of country livin'!"

After working one full hour, the claw reached the blockage and gouged its way through unseen mire. I went inside only to hear Joe call out, "Gracie, would you help me rehang the closet door?"

I met him at the entry hall, and we began our struggle with the complicated door. I stooped to work on the bottom part while Joe attempted to place the top roller back in its track — a difficult task, even on a good day. Joe would get his roller in the track and the bottom pin would bounce out. I'd get the pin at the bottom snug, and Joe's roller would jump the track. Before long, Joe bellowed in exasperation, "Bend closer to the floor so you can see!"

Obediently, I got down on all fours.

"Push to the right," I said. Joe obediently complied. Unfortunately, what I really meant to say was "Push to the left!" When Joe looked down, all he could see was my startled face pinched between the wooden facing and the dangling door.

"You don't love me!" I wailed.

"Yes, I do!" he responded. Then with a wink he added, "Even more than I love our septic system."

Eventually we managed to get the door on track — and my face dislodged and patted to its original shape. Joe changed clothes, then sheepishly grinned as he asked, "How 'bout giving me a hand one more time? Just for fun."

Hand in hand, we bravely marched outside to face "Rooter D-2." Joe placed the robot behind the car's bumper and gave me instructions on how to lift it. Then, with deep feeling in his voice, he put his arms around my shoulders and said, "No matter what happens when we pick this thing up, I do love you."

We put the machine into the trunk without doing bodily injury or emotional harm, and I headed inside to clean up the mess.

If I can just collect my emotions before another disaster strikes, I thought, *I'll be a happy woman.* But lo, it was not to be.

Before I could find the mop, Joe called from the back door, "Gracie, I need you to take me to work. My car won't start!"

You're Never Fully Dressed without a Smile... and Earrings!
Sue Buchanan

Several times a year my friends and I take off together to work. We are creative women of all ages; some of us write books, some music; others teach and plan school and church productions.

On one of these occasions we discovered a whole block of street vendors, one of which had *the most* to-die-for, drop-dead gorgeous jewelry we had ever seen. One of my younger friends — who shall remain nameless for obvious reasons — immediately fell in love with a pair of earrings that cost thirty-five *worth-every-cent-of-it* dollars!

"Buy them! Buy them!" we urged, forgetting for the moment that in order to come on this trip, she had to promise her husband (with her hand on her grandmother's Bible) that she wouldn't spend a penny that wasn't absolutely necessary.

"Oh, let me help you. Let me teach you how to deal with these situations," I said. "Buy the earrings, go home, take off all your clothes, put on the earrings, and ask your husband if he thinks the expense was *absolutely necessary.*" She bought the earrings, we had a good laugh, and I didn't give it another thought.

The next time I saw her husband, he was grinning from ear to ear. For the life of me I didn't know why. Finally I asked.

"You are a great example of an older woman teaching a younger woman," he said. "My wife can go on a trip with you anytime!"

15

A Laugh a Day
Keeps the Doctor Away

*The only way to keep your health is to eat what you don't want,
drink what you don't like, and do what you'd rather not.*

— Mark Twain

*Blessed are those who hunger and thirst, for they
are sticking to their diets.*

— Anonymous

The Hematoma
Marsha Marks

A lot of people say that perception is reality, but I know that sometimes perception has nothing at all to do with reality.

For example, I like to read medical books, and sometimes when I'm reading those books, I begin to imagine I have the disease I'm reading about. I'll read about a disease with symptoms of a tingling big toe, and suddenly my big toe is tingling. It doesn't take much to make the leap from a symptom of the disease to planning my funeral. All based on a false perception.

However, there was one day when the reading of my medical books paid off. On that day I made the alarming discovery of a hematoma on my baby's leg. Mandy was five months old at the time. I'd laid her down for the evening, and when she woke up the next morning, there it was: the ugliest hematoma ever. So dark purple and clotted with blood you could hardly see the skin. It was a quarter inch in diameter and sticking up like a wart. A hematoma is defined in the medical dictionary as "a localized collection of blood, usually clotted in an organ, space, or tissue due to a break in the wall of a blood vessel." I had never seen one this thick with blood and this firm. I bathed Mandy with a sponge, carefully avoiding the hematoma. I was afraid to touch it. When I called the pediatrician's office and told them what was happening, they were sufficiently alarmed to get me in right away.

The expert doctor examined the hematoma from all angles. He swabbed it a few times and studied it some more. Then, to my horror, he began discussing his career and the importance of documenting such an unusual hematoma for the medical records. He spoke of doing a paper on this and getting published and recognized.

I felt I was in some kind of a nightmare in which the mother of the child only wants to know how we are going to prevent future breaks in her daughter's blood vessels and the doctor wants to get famous from the event.

But I was too stunned to protest; when the doctor went to get his camera, I went mute. He came back in and positioned my daughter's leg under the bright lights of the camera. Then he swabbed the hematoma one more time. And it came off. That's when I realized it was a gummy bear. A grape gummy bear. Actually, half of a grape gummy bear. I'd been eating them over my daughter's crib, and apparently I had bit one in half and the other half had gone into the folds of her blanket and adhered to her leg where it had sealed itself by the warmth of her body and hardened as it was exposed to air.

The doctor's warm lights had shone on the leg so long they had softened the hardened candy and revealed it for what it was.

I yelled, "Oh, it's a gummy bear! A grape gummy bear!" The doctor lowered his camera.

I've never seen a red blush of embarrassment rise on a man's face as I saw it rise on the face of that pediatrician.

Nightmare in Second Grade
Phil Callaway

It all began way back in second grade when Miss Barzley came to town. Before Miss Barzley I didn't know how to spell terror. But after her first visit, the very sight of that white Health Department cruiser was enough to send our entire class scattering for seclusion in the nearby woods.

The first time Miss Barzley came to town, we trusted her entirely. And so, like very young lambs, we were lined up single file in a darkened hallway and shot one by one.

I remember standing for the very first time near the back of the line, unsure of the results of reaching the front. Those who had gone on ahead were filing by with "attempted amputation" written all over their voices. "OOOOWWWW!" was how they put it, as they rolled down their sleeves. Oh, how I longed for the hand of my father. He would show Miss Barzley.

But each of us entered The Room dreadfully alone.

Miss Barzley was a rather imposing figure, even without the needle in her hand. Large storehouses of fat (we nicknamed them Lester and Bob) hung like butterballs from her arms as she lifted them upward, squinting at the needle and squeezing a few drops heavenward. Her smile was screwed tightly shut on her humorless face. The glasses on her nose were the thickest I'd ever seen, and she reminded me of a huge insect, a mosquito, I suppose. "Roll up your sleeve. It won't hurt," Miss Barzley lied. Then she poked us. It took just a moment, but we were scarred for life.

Once she finished, she handed me a sugar cube, the reward for not passing out. I tried to take two, but she spotted me with her big eyes and squashed me like a bug.

Twenty-three years later, when my wife informed me that the time had arrived for our son, Stephen, to receive the shot some adult members of our civilized society have decided to give all five-year-olds, I volunteered to take him to the nurse. I was, after all, the obvious choice to comfort him. Having been poked myself, I knew what he was facing. I would hold his hand. Cringe with him. It's something brave fathers do these days.

"Will it hurt, Daddy?" We were on our way to the clinic now, and I had just informed my son of the reason. The tears came quickly as the news shattered his gentle world of cowboy games and toy guns.

"Well, Son," I said, remembering an old lie told me by a young dentist, "it will pinch a little."

"But what will they do?"

"They will put the needle into your arm, and it will come out at your knee."

"Naw." He laughed and began to wipe his tears. Anything Dad jokes about can't be too serious.

"If you are brave, we'll go out for a treat after."

A month has passed. The pain has subsided, but not the memory. Today Stephen and I are on our way to another clinic. Today we will have our warts removed — together. It seems fear is not the only thing he has inherited.

"What will they do?" asks Stephen.

"They will probably have to take our feet off to work on the warts," answers his dad.

"Naw," he laughs.

"Tell you what, Son. I'll be there. Remember, I've got a wart too. And if we are real brave," I say, "we will get a treat after."

At the clinic, Stephen is terrified again. My presence brings little comfort, my words even less.

In the doctor's office we wait. The seasons come and go. Finally the doctor arrives with a bubbling vat of something.

"Sorry I'm late," he says.

"That's okay ... are you sure there isn't something else you should be doing?"

Stephen is looking at the bubbling vat. His eyes are very wide. Like an insect's.

"It's liquid nitrogen," says the doc. "Minus three hundred degrees."

Oh, good, he is going to freeze our feet off!

"You go first, Phil."

"Uh, me? Um, okay, Doctor."

Slowly I remove my sock. He dips a long Q-Tip into the vat and rubs it on my wart. A little boy watches nervously, his eyes darting between my false smile and my afflicted foot. "See, Son, it's gonna be okay."

When Stephen's turn arrives, he is relatively calm. He looks into my face as the doctor dips the Q-Tip. *Daddy can handle it*, the boy is thinking, *so can I.*

Minutes later, we are seated in a nearby restaurant. Our feet are a little tender, but our spirits are good. It's time for our "above and beyond the call of bravery" awards. We have selected the chocolate and raspberry variety. When they arrive, a little boy has some questions.

"Will our warts stay gone?"

"I think so."

"Did yours hurt?"

"A little bit."

"Mine hurt a lot ... but you were there."

As we lick the last of the berries and ice cream, I tell him of Miss Barzley. Of waiting in a darkened hallway to get poked. Of her wobbly arms. Of her big eyes. And of the sharp needles. "Sometimes I wished my dad could be there with me, Stephen."

Stephen has run out of ice cream and is eyeing the pop machine.

"Are you glad Daddy was there today?" I ask him.

"Yep." And then he adds, "I'm glad you got poked."

What Heaven Is Like
Anonymous

An elderly couple were killed in an accident and found themselves being given a tour of heaven by Saint Peter. "Here is your oceanside condo; over there are the tennis courts, swimming pool, and two golf courses. If you need any refreshments, just stop by any of the many five-star restaurants located throughout the area."

"Heck, Gloria," the old man hissed when Saint Peter walked off. "We could have been here ten years ago if you hadn't heard about all that stupid oat bran, wheat germ, and low-fat diets!"

Give the Lord a Challenge in the Rapture
Mark Lowry

ⓔ

Bill Gaither just called. He said he's on a diet and lost fifteen pounds since I've last seen him. I asked, "Did you get a haircut?"

He said, "No, I'm losing weight by eating vegetables." I asked if he was allowed to cook 'em in fatback and bacon. He said, "I don't even like the taste of ham in my green beans anymore." Well, la-di-da!

He went on to tell of the colonic benefits of eating vegetables. We talked about everything from regularity to age spots. It was a pleasant conversation. You know you're officially over forty when you can spend thirty fascinating minutes talking about polyps.

I asked him what he ate today. He said, "A slice of wheat toast in the morning, cottage cheese and fresh tomatoes at noon, then green beans and a salad for dinner."

So I asked him again, "What did you *eat* today?" He repeated himself, which he does often, but it sounded like a snack spread out over the day. While I was talking to Bill, I was looking at the sticky notes on my computer. And then I saw it: a meatless recipe I'd written down and tried. I told Bill I had a dish that would go perfect with his vegetable diet. There is NO MEAT in the following recipe. Not one of God's creatures had to die for us to enjoy this wonderful side dish. Absolutely nothing in the following recipe ever had a mother.

Mark's Remarkable Vegetarian Side Dish

Combine the following:

1 cup self-rising flour

3/4 cup sugar

2 tablespoons cocoa

1 teaspoon vanilla

1/2 cup milk

2 tablespoons margarine (or butter if you laugh in the face of cholesterol)

Pour into baking dish. Mix together and sprinkle 2 tablespoons cocoa and 1 cup sugar on top. Pour 1 1/2 cups of hot water over all. Bake at 350 degrees for 30–40 minutes. Top with homemade vanilla bean ice cream.

I'm glad Bill's lost weight. But have you seen him lately? I don't think anyone should weigh less than their hair. And as padded people (like me) age, we have less wrinkles than skinny people (like Bill). In fact, Bill was commenting about the excess epidermis that hangs around his neck since he's lost weight. He said his grandson, Jess, was sitting on his lap the other day and started playing with his multiple chins. Jess sat quietly as he twisted and pulled on them and finally said, "Papaw, did God make you?"

Bill said, "Yes."

"Did God make me?"

"Yes, he did, Jess."

Jess sat there for a minute and then said, "He's doing a whole lot better these days, isn't he?"

So there you have it. Wanna have grandkids playing with your turkey neck? Lose weight. Wanna give the Lord a challenge in the rapture? Order a pizza. God can handle it.

Nickels and Dimes
Anonymous

A middle-aged woman seemed timid as she visited her gynecologist. "Come now," coaxed the doctor, "you've been seeing me for years! There's nothing you can't tell me."

"This one's kind of strange ...," said the woman.

"Let me be the judge of that," the doctor replied.

"Well," said the woman, "yesterday I went to the bathroom in the morning and I heard a *plink-plink* in the toilet. When I looked down, the water was full of pennies."

"Mmmm, I see," said the doctor.

"That afternoon I went again, and there were nickels in the bowl."

"Uh-huh," the doctor said as he got more and more interested in her story.

"That night," she went on, "there were dimes and this morning there were quarters! You've got to tell me what's wrong with me!" she implored. "I'm scared out of my wits!"

The gynecologist put a comforting hand on her shoulder. "There's nothing to be frightened about. You're simply going through the change."

Laugh Away the Calories
Barbara Johnson

There is nothing like a good belly laugh to lift our spirits, restore our hope, and ease our sorrow. And now scientists realize it's a great weight-loss tool too. I read somewhere that one hundred belly laughs are equal to working out on a rowing machine for ten minutes! (This idea came from the same person who said jumping to conclusions is a great way to boost your heart rate.)

Even though I do my best to laugh my way through every day, I haven't lost any weight doing it. So I'm thinking about starting a new diet I heard about. You can eat all you want ... of everything you don't like! Of course, exercise is important too. But motivation is my problem there. Finally I came up with an incentive for doing sit-ups. I squeeze an ice-cream cone between my knees and take a lick every time I reach for my toes!

Caution: There is a drawback to laughing off too much weight. The problem was illustrated by an old lady in a rest home who told her friend: "It's my birthday. I'm eighty-five years old, and by golly, I want to do something fun today, something shocking. I'm gonna streak through the cafeteria in my birthday suit."

Sure enough, she ran naked through the dining hall. Two old men, leaning over their soup bowls, watched stone-faced as the old gal trotted by. Then one of them commented to the other, "Say, Alma's jogging suit is kinda wrinkled today, isn't it?"

16

Can't Stop Laughing

An onion can make people cry, but there's never been
a vegetable that can make people laugh.

— Will Rogers

One out of four people in this country is mentally unbalanced. Think
of your three closest friends; if they seem okay, then you're the one.

— Ann Landers

The Year's Best Headlines
Anonymous

- Police Begin Campaign to Run Down Jaywalkers
- Experts Say School Bus Passengers Should Be Belted
- Iraqi Head Seeks Arms
- Panda Mating Fails; Veterinarian Takes Over
- Eye Drops Off Shelf
- Teacher Strikes Idle Kids
- Enraged Cow Injures Farmer with Ax
- Plane Too Close to Ground, Crash Probe Told
- Juvenile Court to Try Shooting Defendant
- Two Sisters Reunited After 18 Years at Checkout Counters
- If Strike Isn't Settled Quickly, It May Last Awhile
- Cold Wave Linked to Temperatures
- Red Tape Holds Up New Bridges
- Typhoon Rips Through Cemetery; Hundreds Dead
- New Study of Obesity Looks for Larger Test Group
- Astronaut Takes Blame for Gas in Spacecraft
- Kids Make Nutritious Snacks
- Chef Throws His Heart into Helping Feed Needy
- Local High School Dropouts Cut in Half
- New Vaccine May Contain Rabies

- Hospitals Are Sued by Seven Foot Doctors
- Drunk Gets Nine Months in Violin Case
- Prostitutes Appeal to Pope
- British Left Waffles on Falkland Islands
- Stolen Painting Found by Tree
- War Dims Hope for Peace

Over the Hill So Soon?
James Rahtjen

On my son Luke's sixth birthday, I asked him how he felt. Holding up six outstretched fingers, he replied in all seriousness, "I can't believe I've used up a whole hand already."

Stick with Me, Lord!
Barbara Johnson

What a nightmare I had the other night! In my dream, I was trying to open a little tube of Insty-Stick Super Glue by poking it with a pin. The tube was slick, and I was grasping it tightly when suddenly the end popped open and glue spurted all over my hands!

I quickly grabbed a paper towel — and of course instead of wiping the glue off, the paper towel got stuck to my hands. I wasn't thinking clearly at that point and hurried to the sink to wash off the mess — and promptly got my right hand stuck to the faucet! Wouldn't you know, the phone rang just then. I fumbled as I snatched it off the hook — understandably, since I had to stretch all the way from the sink where my hand was stuck. I guess I got glue all over the phone, because the next thing I knew, my left hand was stuck to the phone, and the phone was stuck to my head! Thanks goodness I woke up at that point, before I managed to permanently weld any other kitchen fixtures to my body!

For a long time I've said that *hope* is the glue that plasters my heart to God. My dream reminded me of how intractable that bond must be. Hope is not like the Post-It note adhesive that can be easily pulled away. Hope is the Insty-Stick Super Glue that coats us with God's tenacious presence forever.

Fun with Phones, Part I: Top Ten Ways to Harass a Telemarketer

Anonymous

10. When they ask "How are you today?" tell them! "I'm so glad you asked because no one these days seems to care, and I have all these problems; my arthritis is acting up, my eyelashes are sore, my dog just died ..."

9. If they say they're John Doe from XYZ Company, ask him to spell his name. Then ask him to spell the company name. Then ask him where it is located. Continue asking him personal questions or questions about his company for as long as necessary.

8. Cry out in surprise, "Judy! Is that you? Oh, my! Judy, how have you been?" Hopefully, this will give Judy a few brief moments of pause as she tries to figure out where she could know you from.

7. If the phone company calls trying to get you to sign up for the Family and Friends plan, reply, in as SINISTER a voice as you can, "I don't have any friends ... would you be my friend?"

6. If they want to loan you money, tell them you are just about to file for bankruptcy and you could sure use some money.

5. Tell the telemarketer you are on "home incarceration" and ask if they could bring you a case of beer and some chips.

4. After the telemarketer gives their spiel, ask him/her to marry you. When they get all flustered, tell them that you couldn't just give your credit card number to a complete stranger.

3. Tell the telemarketer you are busy at the moment and ask them if they will give you their HOME phone number so

you can call them back. When the telemarketer explains that they cannot give out their HOME number, you say, "I guess you don't want anyone bothering you at home, right?" The telemarketer will agree and you say, "Now you know how I feel!"

2. Insist that the caller is really your buddy Leon, playing a joke. "Come on, Leon, cut it out! Seriously, Leon, how's your momma?"

And, first and foremost:

1. Tell them to talk VERY SLOWLY, because you want to write EVERY WORD down.

Fun with Phones, Part II:
The Telemarketing Cure
Phil Callaway

There are times when the telephone is a blessing — when it brings good news, a welcome voice, or some timely advice. But increasingly the phone brings a telemarketer — and often during the dinner hour. This was a problem for us until we got an answering machine. Now if there is an emergency — if, for instance, someone gets their tongue stuck on a flagpole in the winter — we are able to hear them scream through their cell phone and we go to the rescue. If they leave the correct address. Otherwise we continue our dinner-table conversation.

Sometimes I miss those chats with the telemarketers. It's important to remember that they are people too, and that they can be a lot of fun, particularly if you try the following:

Me: Hello?

AT&T: I'd like to speak to Mr. Callaway, please.

Me: Mr. Callaway is my dad. My name is Phil.

AT&T: Can I speak to your dad then?

Me: No, my wife won't let him live here.

AT&T: Um ... Mr. Callaway, we would like to offer you 10 cents a minute, 7 days a week, 24 hours a day.

Me: WOW! THAT'S INCREDIBLE! HOW MUCH IS THAT? *(with hand over receiver now)* HONEY! WE WON!

AT&T: Pardon me?

Me: *(rather excited)* Let me go get a calculator. Just a second ...

AT&T: Uh ... Mr. Callaway —

Me: *(pushing buttons on the calculator)* Amazing! Ten cents a minute for a year is ... let me see ... $52,560. I won't even need to work anymore. Will you send me a check annually or once a month?

AT&T: *click.*

In-Flight Announcements
Anonymous

On a Southwest flight (SW has no assigned seating; you just sit where you want) passengers were apparently having a hard time when a flight attendant announced, "People, people, we're not picking out furniture here; find a seat and get in it!"

"In the event of a sudden loss of cabin pressure, masks will descend from the ceiling. Stop screaming, grab the mask, and pull it over your face. If you have a small child traveling with you, secure your mask before assisting with theirs. If you are traveling with more than one child, pick your favorite."

"Weather at our destination is fifty degrees with some broken clouds, but we'll try to have them fixed before we arrive. Thank you, and remember, nobody loves you, or your money, more than Southwest Airlines."

After a real crusher of a landing in Phoenix, the attendant came on with, "Ladies and gentlemen, please remain in your seats until Captain Crash and the Crew have brought the aircraft to a screeching halt against the gate. And once the tire smoke has cleared and the warning bells are silenced, we'll open the door and you can pick your way through the wreckage to the terminal."

"Ladies and gentlemen, if you wish to smoke, the smoking section on this airplane is on the wing, and if you can light 'em, you can smoke 'em."

17

Laughing All the Way

The cheerful heart has a continual feast.

— Proverbs 15:15

It is God's giving if we laugh or weep.

— Sophocles

Pie in the Sky
Luci Swindoll

Summer in Palm Desert, California, is more than a challenge ... it's a commitment to staying alive. The hottest day I've experienced was 128 degrees. Nothing moves or stirs. The plants don't wither, they're electrocuted — they just turn brown and crumble.

One such day a friend and I decided to go out for dinner after it had cooled off ... to 100 degrees. We looked forward to it all day — our big outing. I picked her up and we ate and visited leisurely, then took dessert to go. A lemon meringue pie. Great choice!

When we got to her house, I asked, "Where's the pie?"

"Oh, gosh. I thought you had it. You were the last one holding it."

We looked in the car, the garage, even the kitchen ... and then I remembered: I'd put the pie on top of the car while I threw my purse in the backseat. Forgetting it was there, we took off.

Piecing all this together we gasped at first, then started laughing. We could picture that pie sailing through the air, and the look of amazement on people's faces as it flew by. Retracing our steps just to satisfy our own curiosity, we found it on the side of the road. Lemon meringue was splattered in gutters and on curbs and sidewalks all along the route. The empty pie pan was leaning against a fire hydrant. We howled!

When life throws you a little curve today, throw it right back with a hearty laugh. This too shall pass. *When the going gets rough, Lord ... give me a laugh. Amen.*

Unmasked!

Patsy Clairmont

An adult cousin disguised herself and stepped into Mom and Dad's house. The only one in the kitchen was my toddler brother, Donnie, who was sitting in his highchair. On seeing a masked person enter the room, he began to cry. The cousin, deciding this wasn't such a good idea after all, bolted out the door and raced down the street for her house.

My mom stepped into the kitchen to see why Don was howling just in time to catch a glimpse of someone dashing out the door. Mom sped for the door in hot pursuit and, being the fleeter of the two, overtook the stranger a block away in a field and tackled her. The cousin was so breathless from the race and subsequent laughter as they scuffled that she couldn't identify herself to Mom before her mask was ripped off. Once my mom discovered who it was, they had a lively chuckle together, but my feisty little mom had made it clear she wasn't about to let any home intruder escape.

Mom's humor surprised me one day when I was fifteen years old. I had just washed my hands in the kitchen sink and was searching for a dishtowel to dry my hands when Mom walked through carrying a load of freshly folded quilts. Feeling fairly safe because her arms were full, I flicked the water from my hands at her, not anticipating her playful response. Before I knew what had happened, Mom dropped the quilts, corralled my head in her arm, and galloped me to the sink, where I got an ample dousing. We both laughed ourselves silly.

Well, That's One Explanation...
Mae H. Fortson

◎

My four-year-old niece, Runa, was delighted with the story of the resurrection, which she asked her mom to repeat over and over. A few days before Easter, she was searching the house for her older brother. Finally, she went into his room, calling his name. Receiving no response, she raised her arms and shouted, "Yahoo, he is not here. He is risen!"

Da Big Chair
Kim Bolton with Chris Wave

God will speak to this people, to whom he said,
"This is the resting place, let the weary rest"; and,
"This is the place of repose" — but they would not listen.
So then, the word of the LORD to them will become:
Do and do, do and do.

Isaiah 28:11–13

Jelly globs beckoned me to release them from their incarceration to my table. I picked the path of least resistance across my kitchen floor, hoping to avoid the toddler cookie-drool that threatened to glue me in place. Unmade beds, dirty dishes, unopened bills, carpool responsibilities, the needs of my family — what about my needs?

From the middle of the screaming piles, a small, sweet voice beckoned. I peered over the edge of the basket I was carrying — laundry mounded past my eyebrows.

"Hey, Mom," he said. "Why don'tcha come and sit wif me in da big chair?"

Balancing my precarious load, I explained to my toddler, "I have too much to do; I can't sit in the big chair or anywhere else, honey."

"Come on, come and sit wight here by me." He patted the space between him and the armrest.

"I can't, baby," I moaned, thinking of the chores that numbered in the legion.

"Come on, now; it'll just take a minute, just a wittle minute." He smiled the irresistible smile of a two-year-old boy. He continued to pat the waiting space next to him.

I dropped my load of laundry. I melted into the seat next to him. And he placed his tiny hand on my face and said, "Now, isn't dis nice, Mom?"

"Yes," I said, "it's wonderful." We sat together for ninety seconds. Then as if he understood the demands waiting for me, he tenderly patted my leg and said, "You can go now."

Just like Jesus. He waits, patting the space next to him, and says, "This is the resting place — next to me."

"Maybe tonight," we say, "maybeafterlunchmaybewhenItakeoutthetrashmaybetonightbeforebedmaybetomorrowafterschoolbeforebed." And it doesn't happen.

He keeps patting.

Jesus keeps patting the space between him and the "next thing," saying, "Just a little minute. A little minute in My Big Chair. It will change your day, probably your life."

"Maybebeforebathtime, bedtime, suppertimemaybemaybe," we drone.

Sit yourself in da big chair. Find your spot in the quiet place. Sit there, so that the Lord doesn't have to say to you, "Okay then, 'do and do, do and do.'"

A "Dee Dah Day"
John Ortberg

Sometime ago I was giving a bath to our three children. I had a custom of bathing them together, more to save time than anything else. I knew that eventually I would have to stop the group bathing, but for the time it seemed efficient.

Johnny was still in the tub, Laura was out and safely in her pajamas, and I was trying to get Mallory dried off. Mallory was out of the water, but was doing what has come to be known in our family as the Dee Dah Day dance. This consists of her running around and around in circles, singing over and over again, "Dee dah day, dee dah day." It is a relatively simple dance expressing great joy. When she is too happy to hold it in any longer, when words are inadequate to give voice to her euphoria, she has to dance to release her joy. So she does the Dee Dah Day.

On this particular occasion, I was irritated. "Mallory, hurry!" I prodded. So she did — she began running in circles faster and faster and chanting "dee dah day" more rapidly. "No, Mallory, that's not what I mean! Stop with the dee dah day stuff, and get over here so I can dry you off. Hurry!"

Then she asked the profound question: "Why?"

I had no answer. I had nowhere to go, nothing to do, no meeting to attend, no sermons to write. I was just so used to hurrying, so preoccupied with my own little agenda, so trapped in this rut of moving from one task to another, that here was life, here was joy, here was an invitation to the dance right in front of me — and I was missing it.

So I got up, and Mallory and I did the Dee Dah Day dance together. She said I was pretty good at it too, for a man my age.

Giving Credit Where Credit Is Due
Lauri Johnson

Recently, I took my sons, twelve-year-old Matthew and six-year-old Ryan, to my parents' house for an afternoon visit. They spent some time playing and socializing with their grandparents. When we were ready to leave, my dad said to Matthew, "You've made my day."

Matthew replied, "God made your day. We just put the icing on it."

Credits

The compilers acknowledge with gratitude the publishers and individuals who granted permission to reprint the stories found within the pages of this book. In a few cases, it was not possible to trace the original authors. The compilers will be happy to rectify this if and when the authors contact them by writing to Zondervan, 5300 Patterson Ave. SE, Grand Rapids, MI 49530. Each piece is noted in the order it appears in the book.

"Wild Mama" by Rachael Phillips. Used by permission. http://home.earthlink.net/~phillips53/rachaelphillips/. For reprint permission contact Rachael Phillips at phillips53@earthlink.net.

"Maybe They're Just Young at Heart" by David L. Reese first appeared in the July/August 2002 issue of *Today's Christian* (formerly *Christian Reader*), a publication of Christianity Today, Inc. Used by permission.

"The Truth Hurts" excerpt by Sally R. first appeared in the Fall 2002 issue of *Christian Parenting Today*, a publication of Christianity Today, Inc.

"Adorable, Schmorable!" is taken from *Scandalous Grace* by Julie Ann Barnhill, published by Tyndale House Publishers. Copyright © 2004. All rights reserved. International copyright secured. Used by permission.

"Oh, Baby!" by Rachael Phillips. Used by permission. http://home.earthlink.net/~phillips53/rachaelphillips/. For reprint permission contact Rachael Phillips at phillips53@earthlink.net.

"'Pledging' Her Love" by Michele Howe first appeared in the January/February 2001 issue of *Today's Christian* (formerly *Christian Reader*), a publication of Christianity Today, Inc. Used by permission.